Artisan Felting
WEARABLE ART

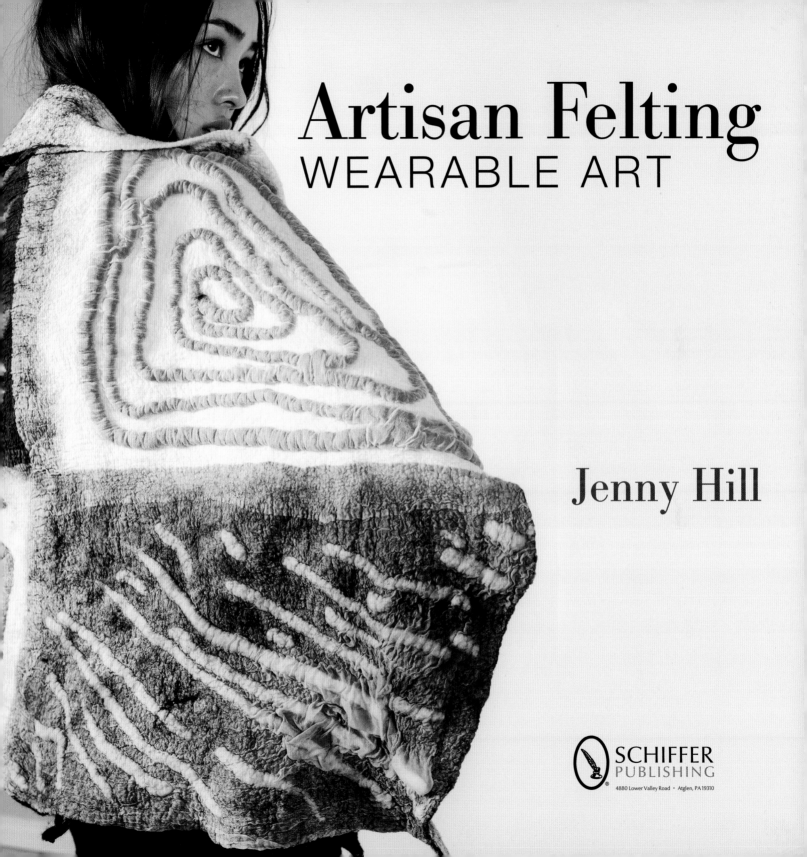

Artisan Felting
WEARABLE ART

Jenny Hill

SCHIFFER
PUBLISHING
4880 Lower Valley Road • Atglen, PA 19310

Other Schiffer Books on Related Subjects:

Felting, Elvira López Del Prado Rivas, ISBN 978-0-7643-4531-9

Fashion Print Design: From Idea to Final Print, Ángel Fernández &
Daniela Santos Quartino, ISBN 978-0-7643-4591-3

Produced by BlueRed Press Ltd. 2019
Designed by Insight Design Concepts Ltd.
Type set in Bodoni

ISBN: 978-0-7643-5852-4
Printed in China

Published by Schiffer Publishing, Ltd.
4880 Lower Valley Road
Atglen, PA 19310
Phone: (610) 593-1777; Fax: (610) 593-2002
Email: Info@schifferbooks.com
Web: www.schifferbooks.com

For our complete selection of fine books on this and related
subjects, please visit our website at www.schifferbooks.com. You
may also write for a free catalog.

Schiffer Publishing's titles are available at special discounts
for bulk purchases for sales promotions or premiums. Special
editions, including personalized covers, corporate imprints, and
excerpts, can be created in large quantities for special needs. For
more information, contact the publisher.

We are always looking for people to write books on new and
related subjects. If you have an idea for a book, please contact us
at proposals@schifferbooks.com.

Contents

Introduction

As a third-generation artist, I grew up spending a lot of time in the fine-art painting studios of my mom and her father. Arts, crafts, sewing projects, and anything creative kept me entertained throughout my childhood. At ten years old, I started designing and creating my own costumes and dresses and various clothing items that were unique and different from what I saw others wearing in school. I wanted to create things that were original—things that hadn't been seen before.

I was introduced to felting in the summer of 2012, among the rolling green hills of Vermont. I had lived in Orange County, California, and worked for nearly a decade in public relations and felt a need for change in my life. Uprooting myself, I embarked on a yearlong adventure as an organic-farm resident and volunteer through a program called World Wide Opportunities on Organic Farms (WWOOF). One of my first farm stays was with a fiber artist and shepherd named Kim Goodling on her family's farmstead, Vermont Grand View Farm.

Not only did Kim become a good friend and an inspiration, but her family's farm also became very special to me. It had sheep, alpacas, a garden, maple trees on tap, an assortment of farm animals, and a border collie. It was also where I learned about nuno felting. Over the summer I spent there, Kim introduced me to felting and fiber arts through her own nuno felt lessons. With no prior exposure to felting. I became mesmerized by the tactile and primitive nature of the medium. To learn it was exhilarating. The possibilities of the combinations and what I could create from this new art appeared endless for me! Hours into the night I sketched felt designs and brainstormed what I would create next.

For the rest of 2012 I stayed at various farms from New England to Tennessee, where I learned how to grow my own food, tend to animals, butcher, make my own clothes, and much more. It was an inspiring, mind-opening, and thought-provoking experience that led me to envision a new kind of future for myself. However, during that year I continued to immerse myself in all the reading material I could find about sheep breeds and the felting process. I visited sheep and wool festivals, and sheep farms around the US, learning all I could about fiber and felting. I would do felt projects in whatever space I could find on the farms where I stayed, and would experiment with the different types of fiber I collected from sheep. It was a simple and magical time in my life. And over the course of that year, my fascination with felting intensified. I spent my days farming and my nights felting and dreaming about what I could make next. I was enchanted by this ancient craft—it became my obsession! I wasn't sure when or how, but I knew I wanted felting to play a central role in my future.

When my WWOOFing year ended in 2013, I moved near my family in Boise, Idaho. But instead of returning to my former public-relations career, I decided that I needed to do the thing that literally kept me up at night: felting. It was an uncertain and risky decision, but I had an uncontrollable urge to follow through. With a weird mixture of confidence and trepidation, I marched down to the Boise City Hall and registered my first-ever company, J. Hill Felt. I started out small, just selling my work at the Boise Farmers Market every Saturday, and at regional art and craft fairs. However, after selling everything I created that year and exceeding my sales goals, the following year I started going to bigger art and fashion trade shows. As my craft improved, so did the demand for my work.

Today, I sell my work internationally to sophisticated and bold women through art and fashion trade shows, as well as through private showings. I am deeply grateful that I get to do what I love every day and am able to share my passion with others.

Why I am writing this book

Over the past decade felting has enjoyed a marked increase in popularity all around the world. However, not everyone has access to a local felting community where they can take workshops to learn and improve their craft. This book is my attempt to reach distant felters and to help those wanting to get better. In it, I answer many questions that felters have asked me over the years, and elaborate on my own discoveries in this medium.

This is the felter's guidebook that I wished existed when I first learned how to felt! It is also a guide for experienced felt makers wanting to improve their skills and learn new felting techniques.

As a resource guide, this book uses nuno-felting techniques to make beautiful and functional clothing and accessories. Through seven tutorial-guided projects, you will learn over thirty specific techniques and approaches to nuno felting. This book will ignite your creativity, inspiring your own nuno-felted wearable-art designs.

In each project I address what makes my designs unique. Every garment is a wearable piece of art created with thought and intention. In addition to technique, I write about color, texture, drape, fit, and the overall flow of the piece. I address some design and fashion rules I follow—and others I have made up along the way. I explore the flexibility of felt and how there are endless ways to achieve your desired outcome.

I hope you enjoy your experience working through this book as you learn new approaches to felt, and that these designs will be enjoyable to construct and inspire your own creativity.

Happy felting!

GETTING STARTED
AND THE BASICS

Studio Setup

My studio is a haven for creative expression. It evolves and moves around too. In seven years, I have had five semipermanent studios. When I first attempted a textile art career, I began felting in a utility closet in my parents' house. After proving to myself that I could make it in the industry, I upgraded to a cute storefront studio rental in a small town near Boise, Idaho. After a year of renting a storefront, then getting married and welcoming kids into the world (twins), I realized the necessity of having a studio inside my home, so I could maintain a balanced lifestyle.

I have moved around a lot because of my own adventures and my husband's career. With all of these location changes, I have been able to create at my full capacity in the various studios that I've made. Because felting has such basic components, I have also been able to travel with my work packed in suitcases and create "satellite studios," from my Textile Art Residency at the Textile Art Center in Iceland to peaceful retreats at my family's mountain cabin in Idaho.

Creating at various inspiring places and living abroad has deeply impacted my work. Now, my current studio is in southern Germany, where my family and I reside.

From all my studio locations, I have learned there are some essentials for a good work space, regardless of where you set up shop. You can starting out using your kitchen table as your creation space—or a utility closet—whichever works! The felting must begin somewhere, and you can adapt many spaces for your studio.

There are many ways to set up a good and productive studio. Make it a positive, inviting space that makes you happy and inspires your creativity.

Here, however, are some important studio elements to ultimately aim for:

• **Access to water** in a studio allows you to easily fill up felt water dispensers and dye pots. Also, easy access to a drain is important for pouring out wastewater.

• **Well-lit spaces**, preferably by natural light, will help you see the details in your work process and in the finished product. It makes for a happy environment too.

• **Properly ventilated** areas are crucial, since you'll be working with a lot of damp surfaces. Plenty of air circulation can prevent mildew, mold, and bad smells. If you dye indoors, good ventilation is an absolute must.

• **Sufficient room** to accommodate all of your felting materials and tools, including a 5 × 7 ft. felting table, plus adequate room for you to work easily around the table. I have worked in smaller spaces and laid out my work in sections rather than on a large surface area—this is possible, but go for the largest suitable space you can get.

• **Noncarpeted flooring** that does not absorb water—such as wood, linoleum, tile, cement, etc.

• **A well-organized space** with materials and tools assigned to designated areas will help your productivity enormously. There should be storage shelves for your materials, tools, and patterns.

• **An inspiring atmosphere** you will enjoy working in. Create your space with thoughtful organization, pleasing décor, inspirational quotes, a vision board, etc. I like to collect sheep artwork as mascots for my studio.

Felting Glossary

Acid dye: A synthetic dye that mainly dyes protein fibers (animal fibers), using hot water and vinegar, or citric acid, as a mordant (bonding agent).

Bubble mat: A bubble-textured plastic surface used for laying out nuno felt. The kind of bubble plastic used in packaging or a pool cover are good materials that provide gentle friction to the wool when it is rubbed and rolled against the bubble surface.

Dry-felting: Lightly vibrating your hands over a wool layout to bond the wool fibers and nuno fibers together before the wet-felting stage. During this process, check and feel for weak spots in the layout.

Dust layer: A layer of wool that is half to a quarter as thick as the base roving layer. It is used to cover up inconsistencies in the layout and to bond seams together.

Extracting water: The final stages of felt where water is spun out of the felt piece with a dedicated felt spin dryer.

Fulling: The later felting process of rubbing, rolling, kneading, and agitating fibers, to further fuse the wool fibers together into a solid material.

Hand-felting tools: To speed up the felting process, hand-felting tools are used to create more friction when rubbing the fibers down. Hand-felting tools also protect your hands from overabrasion and prolonged exposure to water and soap.

Nuno felt: The word "nuno" is Japanese for cloth and refers to entangling wool fibers and a cloth material together through the wet-felting process. Natural and open-weave materials work best for nuno felting.

pH: A chemical unit used to measure the acidity or alkalinity in a given substance. In the felting and dyeing process, understanding the basics of pH is important for opening up the scales of the fibers for entanglement and for dyeing. This leads to achieving the right pH for bonding color to the felt fibers.

Resist: A plastic barrier placed between the felt layers, laid out to prevent the layers from felting together. Resists are used when creating seams and making 3-D felt forms.

Rolling: A stage of felting used to further agitate and bring the fibers together to form felt. Laid-out fibers are rolled up in a bubble mat, secured with ties, and rolled back and forth from elbow to palm.

Roving: Fibers that have been cleaned, combed, and carded. The fibers are combed out, then straightened in one direction, so they can be easily pulled apart for felting.

Rubbing: Creating friction on a felt layout, using hands, hand-felting tools, or a surface with friction. This action is combined with water and soap to initiate the bonding of fibers.

Saturating fibers: A process of gently distributing water across the surface of a felt layout to begin the rubbing and agitating stages.

Scales: Individual wool fibers are covered with small scales that when agitated and saturated in soap and water open up, interlock, and bond together permanently to create a solid felt material.

Sealing the edges: Wool fibers migrate after they are laid out, saturated, and agitated. Smoothing out the fibers with your palm and fingers will realign the edges back in a straight line.

Sheen: The light or gleam reflected off the fiber's surface.

Shrink factor: The amount of shrinkage from the felt layout to the final fulled garment. (See "Shrink Rates," pages 26–27, for the formula.)

Weak spots: Places on the layout that have holes or light/thin layers, inconsistent with the rest of the layout.

Wet felting: The process of using water, soap, and agitation to entangle and bond wool fibers permanently together into a solid felt material.

Wool batt: Carded wool fibers that have been processed into sheets. The wool fibers are multidirectional and have a consistent thickness.

Wool locks: The individual, unprocessed, clustered strands of fiber on the fleece of a sheep or other fiber animal.

Nuno-Felting Tools and Supplies

Felting tools are basic and easily procurable. With time and practice, you will discover your own preferences and build up your collection of "must have" tools for felting. Let's start with the basics.

Basic Felting Tools

Soap: Most felters have a favorite soap, since they must work with it frequently. Soap with a pH of 7–9 is needed for felting: this type of soap will change the pH of the fibers, causing the scales to open up and interlock. Most dish soaps fall within this pH category. (If you are unsure about the pH, you can contact the soap manufacturer or look it up on the internet.) Using a colorless soap with low suds, low scent, and minimal to no skin irritants will yield the best results. Having incredibly sensitive skin myself, I use an olive oil soap bar that I rub over the top of my wet projects, secured with netting. However, I have been known to use whatever I can find in my studio if I'm in a pinch.

Water dispenser: I have two methods for dispensing water over my felt projects.

First method: I take an empty vinegar bottle (with a screw-top lid) and poke five to eight holes in the lid with a nail. This creates an excellent waterspout. Make sure you poke the holes from the inside of the lid and out. This helps with the water flow—if you do it from the outside in, the water will get jammed. This allows for quick water dispersion when wetting a large surface area.

Second method: Sometimes I start wetting down the layout with a garden/houseplant spray pump, the kind often used for pesticides. Note that this pump should be exclusively used for felting water only. The garden spray pump method has a gentler, more uniform water spray and won't move your loosened fibers around, but it does takes longer. After I put a light layer of water on the wool with the water spray pump, I finish the rest with the vinegar water bottle.

Basic sewing kit: For closing up holes / weak spots and simple adjustments, also sewing on buttons. I just use an ordinary needle and thread.

Bubble mat: Packaging bubble mat is my favorite surface material for nuno felt projects because it is gentle yet provides light friction during the fulling and rolling. I also use a soft, pool-cover bubble mat for heavier projects.

Bubble mat ties: Recycled pantyhose, knee-highs, and cut-up stretchy materials are useful to secure projects in the felt mat when rolled up.

Crochet hook: I use a variety of crochet hook sizes to pull up texture and curls on fur felt pieces.

Felt needles with sponge: For repair work, such as tacking on loose pieces of fiber or closing up a hole.

Felting table: It is important to get a table that is the right height for you and has enough surface area to accommodate large projects. I currently use three tables from IKEA that I can separate or push together, as well as adjust the height. The tables are each 63 in. long × 31 in. wide × 35 in. tall. You can order custom felt tables with gutters and drains in various sizes and heights.

Iron: In the final stages of felting, irons help shape and smooth any creases in the felt.

Mannequin: Choose a mannequin with a similar size to you or the person you are creating the piece for. I shape my final pieces with steam on a mannequin. On fabric-based mannequins, make sure the piece has been fully spun so it is only damp and not dripping any water.

Netting: An open-weave plastic net should be used to cover your project to keep your fibers from shifting when rubbed. The plastic netting is thicker than tulle, but thinner than a plastic window screen.

Palm washboard felters: One of my favorite felting hand tools is Heart Felt Silk's Palm Washboard. Harry and Robbin Firth create more than ten variations of palm washboards, which are handmade with a beautiful variety of woods. These are ergonomically designed and very easy to use. In my felting projects, I use the original, deep, mini, and mini wedge palm washboards. These washboards speed up and improve the felting process. Also, they keep your hands off the soap surface, require less agitation from your hands, and thus cause less irritation from the soap.

Resist pattern plastic: To create the pattern template resist material, I recommend using 6 mm painters' plastic. For a resist material to use between coat flaps, pockets, and other folds, use a thinner painters' plastic or even a cut-up garbage bag.

Rolling rod: For rolling-felt projects, I use 1.5 in. electric pipe or PVC pipe. You can also use a pool noodle. I prefer the sturdiness and the thinness of the electric pipe over the pool noodle; however, both do the job.

Scissors: I use a dry set of sharp, well-maintained scissors for cutting fabrics and dry wool. I use another pair, not as sharp or well maintained, for cutting wet materials. After cutting wet materials, be sure to dry the scissors off to keep them from rusting. For cutting pattern plastic and other materials such as metallic embellishments, I use all-purpose scissors.

Sewing tape measure: To take body measurements for creating patterns, I use a standard sewing tape measure. Tape measures are also very important for the final fulling phase when finalizing the size and shape of the piece.

Sketchbook: Almost all of my designs start with a sketch. A small or large sketchbook is good for planning designs. Sketching may be intimidating for some; however, your sketch doesn't have to be perfect—it is really for you, giving you a place to communicate your ideas, and inspiration for your designs.

Spin dryer: Another name for this is the Laundry Alternative Spin Dryer. Without agitating the fibers, this extracts a lot of water in seconds from felting projects. The spin cycle on a washer can be used—however, it can agitate your work too much, plus it takes several minutes to complete the spin cycle. The purpose-designed spin dryer gives you more control over how much water you extract and how quickly.

Steamer: For shaping and fulling projects—steamers help these processes.

Table risers: For a simple way to add height to a basic folding table, you can cut up 1 in. PVC or electric pipe (make sure to measure your table leg width before you purchase the pipe) and attach these pieces to the foot of each table leg to raise it up by however many inches you need.

Dyeing Tools

When dyeing fabric and fibers, be sure to use dyeing equipment exclusively for dyeing only, to avoid food contamination.

Gloves: Use thick rubber construction gloves for massaging material in the hot pot and checking on the dyeing process. For measuring and mixing dyes outside the pot, use latex or thin plastic gloves.

Measuring spoons: For accuracy, I measure most of my dye powder in 1/8-teaspoon increments.

Mixing cup: A plastic or glass recycled container is used for mixing powder with hot water outside the dye pot.

Portable stove burners: I prefer electric stove units because they are safe for both indoor and outdoor use.

Protein fiber dye / acid dye: These dyes will color both wool and silk combinations or protein fibers. (For cellulose fibers such as cotton or bamboo, use fiber reactive dyes.) I like stocking Jaquard or Ashford acid dyes in the primary colors (red, yellow, and blue) and then mixing them for a wider range of colors. My other color staples are a deep black, navy blue, royal blue, dark brown, and silver. For specialty colors that are harder to mix, I like emerald, lilac, fuchsia, and khaki.

Stainless-steel pots: This material produces the least amount of interference in the dye process. Pots come in a wide variety of sizes. My favorite size is 35 quarts. I know—it's big!

Stirring spoon: A long wooden spoon is used for stirring in and for dissolving dye in the pot.

Vinegar: Basic distilled white vinegar is used for increasing the dye bath pH and also allows the dyes to bond to the fibers.

Fiber Materials

Nuno Material: For the nuno materials I combine with wool roving, I use pongee/habotai (also habutai) silk, silk gauze, silk chiffon, and silk organza. I also like using lightweight cotton material. I often order bolts of undyed material that I can dye myself. I particularly love shopping at specialty fabric stores for beautiful patterned and embroidered fabrics. As long as the fabric is a natural material with a weave open enough to see with the naked eye, it will felt. I also use some synthetic materials with open weaves that take a little more care and time to felt completely.

Assorted yarn: To add embellishments to the surface design of your projects, yarn can add some interesting texture and color. Natural-fiber yarns such as wool, silk, and cotton will felt easily to the surface of your wool. You can use synthetic yarns too, if you cover the yarn with a dust layer of wool.

Silk roving: For extra shine and texture on the surface of my projects, I enjoy using tussah silk, mulberry silk, and silk hankies.

Wool batts: For thicker nuno felts, such as rugs, I use wool batts to save time in the layout and fulling.

White silk habotai

White silk organza

4.5 mm white silk gauze

White textured-silk chiffon

White textured-silk gauze

Cream cotton lace

Silk gauze with embroidered sequins

Golden brown French cotton lace

Black-and-white cotton lace

Wool locks: I source a variety of raw wool locks from small farmers, both local and abroad. I ensure the farmers are skilled at raising sheep for fiber quality and have very few burrs, sticks, vegetation, or feces in the fiber. I usually buy these locks around sheering season in the spring and fall.

Wool prefelt: Prefelt (or needlepunch) is useful when cutting up defined shapes in nuno designs. It can also speed up the felting process. But make sure your prefelt is of the same quality and fineness as your roving or it will create an imbalance.

Wool roving: The majority of the wool roving I use on my projects is undyed 19-micron fine merino. I also use dyed 19-micron fine merino wool roving. Fine wool is the best medium for fibers to migrate through the weave of the nuno materials.

Cashmere raw locks

Wensleydale raw fiber locks

Tussah silk roving

Mohair roving

Textured wool yarn

19-micron undyed merino wool roving

Dyed light-gray 19-micron merino wool roving

Dyed gray 19-micron merino wool roving

Merino wool natural gray roving, 22 micron

Camel roving

Alpaca roving

Basic Wool Layout and Instructions

What Is Nuno Felting?

Nuno felting is a modern take on felting, an ancient textile creation process. Felting is one of the oldest known textile techniques, originating in many Asian and European cultures, particularly from Mongolia, Turkey, Iran, and Russia.

Nuno felting is a way of entangling and compressing layers of wool fibers through a woven fabric base. It requires less wool than traditional wet felting, since the woven fabric acts as a strengthening base. Nuno felting creates a lightweight, durable fabric that can vary in thickness from light, airy scarves to solid winter coats. The nuno material reinforces the strength of the felt, whether thin or dense.

The nuno-felting technique was developed in about 1992 by fiber artist Polly Stirling, from New South Wales, Australia. "Nuno" means cloth in Japanese and represents the material that integrates and felts with the wool-roving fibers when agitated. Nuno materials felt best when they are open-weave natural fibers such as silk, wool, or cotton. However, synthetic fibers with an open weave can also be used; it just requires more patience and time to felt.

Basic Felting Steps

There are five basic steps to creating felt:

1) Wool layout

2) Water, soap, and rubbing

3) Rolling, agitating, and fulling

4) Rinsing and spinning

5) Shaping

(Refer to the sections on tools, pages 16–21, for all tools needed in the following steps.)

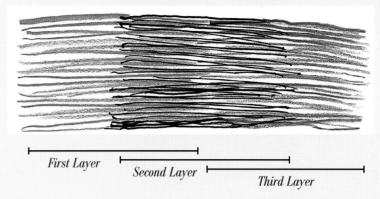

First Layer

Second Layer

Third Layer

Wool Layout

To lay out wool, start by holding the wool roving in your nondominant hand and pull off a fine layer at the top of the roving with your dominant hand. Each layer should be transparent enough to see through when the layer is held up near your eye.

To pull the wool off, place the tips of the wool in the base of your palm and pull the edges with your fingertips. With your nondominant hand holding the wool roving, your grip of the wool should be loose enough to allow the wool piece to glide off, but firm enough to control the fineness of the layer you

Wool roving is cleaned and combed-out wool fibers. It comes in long strands and pulls apart easily.

are pulling off. You should never clench the roving. Practice will allow you to perfect your grip and layout consistency.

Place the wool roving in an up-and-down direction on your nuno felt surface. The layout is made by building up several fine layers of roving. Each layer of roving should overlap in the middle of the previously laid piece of roving.

If you are right-handed, lay your wool from left to right. Vice versa if you are left-handed. This will keep your layers looking clean and even.

It is important to keep the wool layers consistent, whether they are thin or thick. Wool shrinks at different rates according to layout thickness. So, to keep the garment's size consistent with relatively even proportions, you need to keep the layers consistent. (Refer to section "Shrink Rates: Direction of Wool Layout," pages 26–27.)

Vertical and horizontal shrink rates will vary somewhat with nuno felt because of the woven cloth used, and the direction that the wool is laid. When laying in one direction in nuno felting, the vertical and horizontal shrink rates are not as dramatic as in classic felting, which has a one-directional layout without the cloth. You can make up for this horizontal and vertical difference during the fulling process by fulling the horizontal direction more than the vertical direction (this is all explained later).

Using this directional-layout method, there will be more give and stretch in the horizontal direction than in the vertical direction of the final felted piece. This give will be beneficial in shaping around body curves such as the breast, hips, and buttocks.

Though there are different layout methods for nuno felt, for this entire book, I focus mainly on laying the wool in one direction along the contours of the body and the pattern.

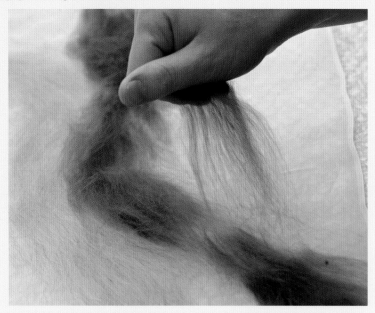

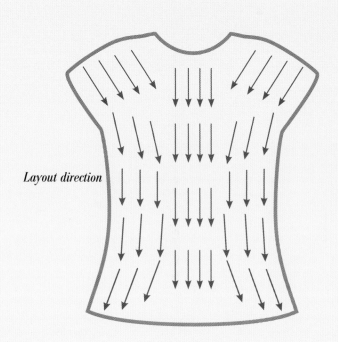

Layout direction

Water, Soap, and Rubbing

When the layout is complete, start saturating the design with water. You should evenly disperse the water and avoid making puddles. After the project is saturated, gently place a plastic net over the top to secure the wet wool layout. Put soap on the netting so it will seep through onto the project. Next, agitate the project with your hands or a felting tool such as the palm washboard. Remove the net after rubbing is complete.

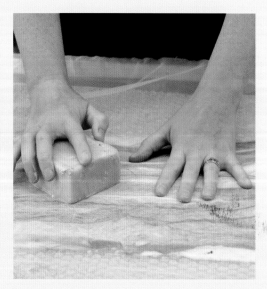

Rolling, Agitating, and Fulling

After the project has been agitated by hand and the felting tool, roll it up in the bubble mat and secure the rolled-up mat with ties. One roll is back and forth along the length of your arm from elbow to fingertips. After rolling, fulling is the next stage.

Fulling is a felt-making term for the process in which the piece becomes solid through agitating the fibers and shrinking them down. This process is done by rubbing the fibers against the bubble mat and then lightly tossing, kneading, and rolling specific areas. The felt piece will become firm and dense during this stage.

Rinsing and Spinning

After the project has been agitated and fulled to completion, rinse out all of the soap and extract the water with a felt spinner.

A felt spinner or Laundry Alternative Spin Dryer gently extracts water from felt without agitating the fibers. Refer to pages 16–21 for more information.

Shaping

This is the final stage, when the piece is shaped and dried. Gently stretch and shape the piece to its final shape, both on and off a mannequin. Rub it around the curves of the mannequin to better define the shape. Iron and apply steam to improve the shaping and setting process.

This is a basic outline of instructions for felting. I will explain and expand on these processes in the seven projects in this book.

Shrink Rates

To create a pattern for each project, you have to consider a few factors about the garment, such as what kind of fit you want on the body, the final weight of the fabric, and how the piece will be worn. To get a very precise fit for a specific body, you must take measurements and account for the felting shrink rate of your layout.

My nuno felt clothing projects will shrink anywhere between 25 to 50 percent from the design layout to the final garment. This is a considerable variation of shrinkage that depends on many things, including the type of wool used, the thickness and consistency of the layout, the direction of wool layout, the type of nuno materials incorporated (silk, cotton, embellishments, etc.), the pressure used to felt and full, the duration of felting the piece, and the water temperature used.

Type of wool used: As a foundation layer for my nuno felt, I use mostly fine merino wool roving with a micron count of 18–19 (depending on the country of origin I am buying from). I use this wool because the thinness of the fibers work easily through the weave of the nuno material. Also, fine wool will felt quickly and is soft against the skin. Most thick wools will shrink less and at a slower rate. These factors should be accounted for in your pattern creation in addition to the sheep breed, color, coarseness, and length of wool fibers.

Type of nuno material used: The weight, openness of weave, and type of material (cotton, silk, synthetic, etc.) will play a big role in how the final material will look, and how much the layout will shrink. Thicker nuno materials such as cotton laces tend to shrink less. The rule is that the finer the material, the more it will shrink with the wool in the layout.

Layout thickness and consistency: The thicker the wool is laid out, the less it will shrink. The thinner the wool layout, the more the wool will shrink.

Wool fibers want to come together and tangle when laid out. The finer the wool layout, the more the wool must gravitate to reach the other fibers to connect, thus creating more shrinkage. If some areas of your layout are finer than others, they will shrink more, which could give a puckered look and unevenness to the finished garment. This principle can be used intentionally or occur by mistake. For example, I will lay an additional layer of wool on my hems and jacket collars to create more structure, weight, and rigidity and cause less shrinkage. I also play with different textures on garments by varying the layout for a crinkly textured look on finer laid-out areas.

Unintentionally, I have also ended up with the front of a dress being 4 inches shorter than the back side because of a heavier layout on the back. It created a new effect that I could implement (on purpose) in future designs, although it wasn't a happy surprise at the time. With layout practice, you can intentionally create a variety of shrink effects or prevent any inconsistencies in layout.

Direction of wool layout: Wool will generally shrink in the direction it is laid out and the direction it is fulled. To create more shrinkage in one direction, such as for a waistline, lay the wool in a horizontal fashion on the waistline to create a silhouette. Also, in the fulling process, you can full specific areas in the direction you want them to shrink.

Use and wear: When creating garments such as a coat that will receive more wear and usage, it is best to use a thicker wool layout to create a dense, airtight, and durable material. You can blend coarser wool breeds with finer breeds to give a stronger shell for the outer layer. This combination of fibers will influence how much the coat will shrink. When creating a lighter-weight garment that will be worn directly against the skin, wool layers will be light and have a larger shrink factor.

Duration, direction, and intensity of fulling: Shrinking amounts will vary based on how much you full a particular area on the garment. For example, I will full the neckline more than any other part so as to make the wool fibers more compact; this makes it structural, so it stands on its own. Other areas of the garment are not fulled for as long; however, they are still fulled tightly and have less rigidity and more flow and drape when worn.

How long you full a piece, the direction you agitate it, and how much pressure you use while fulling greatly influences the shrink rate. For example, if you lightly toss, as opposed to slam, the felt project against the felt table, the latter will cause the fibers to shrink quicker, but in a less controlled way than the former.

Temperature of water: In the initial phases of nuno felting, it is best to use lukewarm water. Water that is too hot causes the wool to shrink rapidly onto other wool fibers without actually felting onto the nuno material fibers. The heat of water used in felting activates the fibers to entangle and shrink together faster. However, toward the end of the fulling phase, after the wool and nuno fibers have been fused together, hot water can be used to speed up the fulling process.

How to Calculate the Shrink Factor by Using Samples:

To accurately estimate how much each project layout will shrink and the fabric weight, look, and feel, you need to do a test sample. This will also help you determine the shrink factor, how much wool to use on your project, and how to lay the wool out.

When creating a sample, you should start with a 10 × 10 in. layout or larger, to get an accurate sense of how the material will look in the final garment. Any smaller and it is harder to see the details. Lay out the wool, nuno material, and any embellishments exactly as you plan to lay them in your final piece. Also, felt the piece the exact way you plan to felt your final garment. When the sample is finished, you can assess whether you like the sample look or whether you need to add or subtract wool layers for the final layout.

Shrink Factor

The pattern you create will reflect the body measurements multiplied by the shrink factor: the amount of shrinkage from layout to the final fulled garment. Below is the shrink factor formula.

For every measurement taken of the body for a felting template, you will multiply by the shrink factor obtained from your sample. For the layout techniques to create a sample, see overleaf.

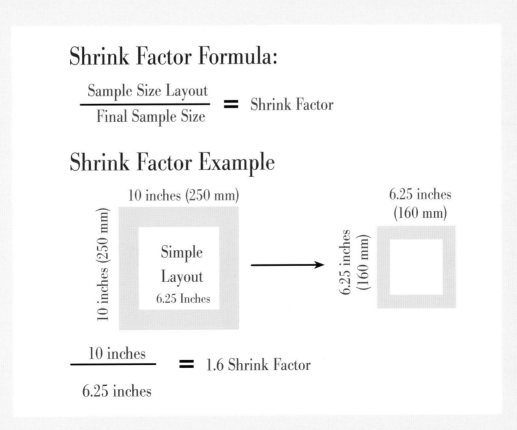

Shrink Factor Formula:

$$\frac{\text{Sample Size Layout}}{\text{Final Sample Size}} = \text{Shrink Factor}$$

Shrink Factor Example

10 inches (250 mm)

10 inches (250 mm)

Simple
Layout
6.25 Inches

6.25 inches
(160 mm)

6.25 inches
(160 mm)

$$\frac{10 \text{ inches}}{6.25 \text{ inches}} = 1.6 \text{ Shrink Factor}$$

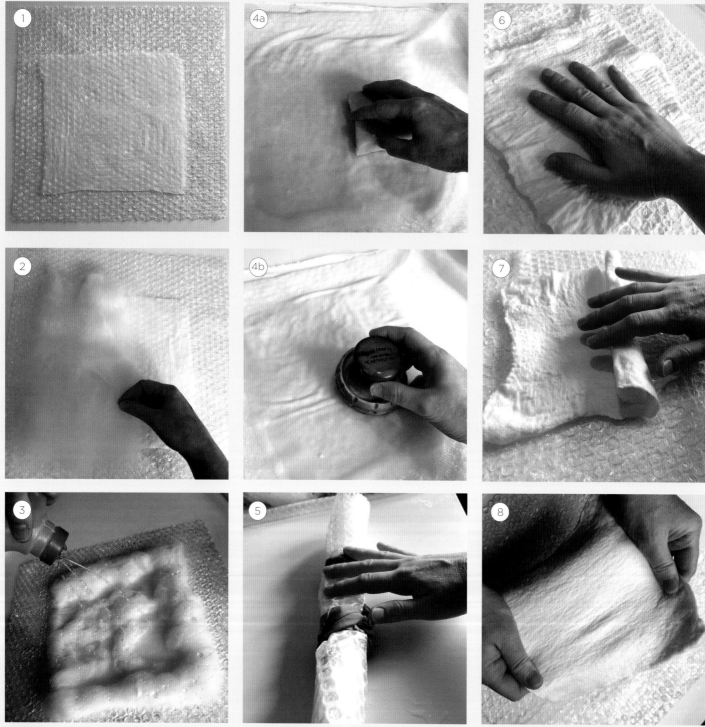

Creating a Sample

1) Measure 10 × 10 in. nuno material onto a bubble mat surface that measures around 15 × 15 in. This size of mat surface will allow you to roll the small sample piece up with ease.

2) Lay wool out in one direction, up and down. You can lay multiple layers or one single fine layer, depending on your desired final fabric weight. If unsure of the weight, it would be best to create three samples side by side all with different thicknesses: light, medium, and heavy.

3) Sprinkle water lightly on top of the surface. You want to fully saturate the wool and silk without creating puddles. After wetting it, tuck the wool and seal it in at the edges, creating a straight crease. This will keep the fibers from splaying out during the rubbing and fulling phase.

4) Cover the piece with a felting net, apply soap, and gently rub with a hand-felting tool or your hands. It should take around five minutes of rubbing in a horizontal and vertical direction to bring the fibers together.

5) Roll the sample piece up in the bubble mat in the direction the wool was laid, fasten it with stretch ties, and roll it about a hundred times. One roll is from your palm to your fingertips and back to your palm. Unroll. Rotate your sample 90°, then roll it back up and repeat a hundred rolls. Then unroll it again.

6) Full your sample piece by rubbing both sides against the bubble surface in a perpendicular direction to the layout, then in the direction of the layout.

7) Roll up the piece in both horizontal and vertical directions and roll it twenty-five times in each direction, one at a time, until you notice significant shrinking. If you notice a big difference in one side of the layout, full in that direction until it shrinks to a similar size.

8) Stretch the sample piece in both directions to even out the horizontal and vertical sides and to smooth out the puckering in the felt. Continue to full until you feel the felt becoming solid, with very few loose fibers seen or felt on the surface. When you press your fingers on the felt piece, it should no longer feel squishy or loose.

Rinse all the soap out and pat it dry with a towel.

Shape the final piece by stretching it in the desired direction.

Iron your sample to flatten it out.

9) Measure your felt sample piece(s). Attach noted measurements to the piece of felt for future reference, such as the before-and-after vertical and horizontal measurements. Also, calculate the shrink factor on your sample.
The sample should be around the same size both vertically and horizontally. If there is a drastic difference, you will have different horizontal and vertical shrink factors. If the sides differ but are very close, average out the lengths of the two sides. On my sample notes for future reference, I describe the layers of wool used (light, medium, heavy), the type of nuno material used, and anything else I want to reference about the creation process.

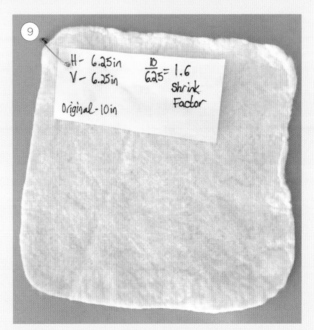

Pattern Template Creation

Taking the Measurements

The measurement tables below represent the main measurements necessary for creating a template pattern. You can copy these blank tables and fill them in with your own measurements for each pattern. After filling in the measurement tables, you can tape them to your own patterns with clear, waterproof tape to easily reference the measurements for each pattern.

Horizontal Measurements:

Each side of the pattern template represents half of the horizontal body measurements, multiplied by the shrink factor. Measure each of the horizontal body circumferences represented in the chart below, then multiply by the shrink factor and divide by two, to get the final template measurement. Round each measurement up or down to the nearest quarter (for example: 13.725 will round up to 13.75).

Formula:

(Horizontal Body Measurement × Shrink Factor) / 2 = Horizontal Template Measurement

Horizontal Measurements Pattern Name: Pattern Size: Shrink Factor:	Body Measurement / Final Garment Measurement	Template Measurement (Body Measurement × Shrink Factor) / 2
Neck circumference (at top of garment)		
Neck circumference (at collarbone)		
Shoulder circumference		
Shoulder-to-armpit circumference		
Bicep circumference		
Elbow circumference		
Lower-arm circumference (between elbow and wrist)		
Wrist circumference		
Bust circumference (at nipple line)		
Under-bust circumference		
Waist circumference		
Hip circumference		
Buttocks circumference		
Circumference at base of garment		

When measuring horizontally, keep in mind how loose or fitted you want the piece to be. Measure with the tape exactly how you want the piece to fit next to the body. For example, you may want to include extra inches of space in the armpit to allow free arm movement. If you are constructing a coat, perhaps you want extra inches of room for a sweater worn underneath. You can play with the dimensions and shape of the sleeves, collars, etc. If you want the garment to be very tailored and snug, keep the measurements closer to the body size.

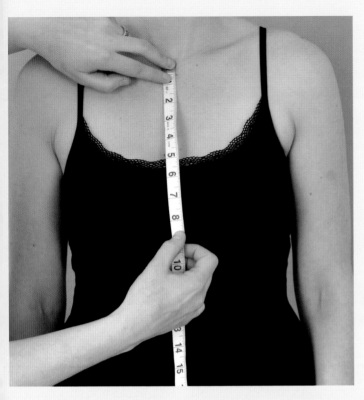

Vertical Body Measurements:

Vertical measurements represent the length of the body part listed below. Each vertical measurement corresponds to the horizontal measurements. Because these are vertical body measurements, they only need to be multiplied by the shrink factor to get the final template measurement.

Formula:

(Vertical body measurement × shrink factor) = Vertical Template Measurement

Note: There are some exceptions regarding shrink rates on the patterns. For example, armholes and necklines may need special consideration. The wool at these openings tends to get stretched more than the wool on the inner layers. I account for this difference by laying the wool at any opening (such as a neckline) in a perpendicular direction to the main layout. I will also lay an additional thin layer of wool at these areas to decrease the stretching and create more structure and weight.

Vertical Measurements	Body Measurement	Template Measurement (Body Measurement × Shrink Factor)
Neck height (measured from collarbone)		
Collarbone to bust/nipple line		
Collarbone to under bustline		
Collarbone to waistline		
Collarbone to hipline		
Collarbone to buttocks line		
End of shoulder to armpit		
End of shoulder to elbow		
Elbow to wrist (allow extra inches for a cuff if desired)		
Collarbone to final length of garment		

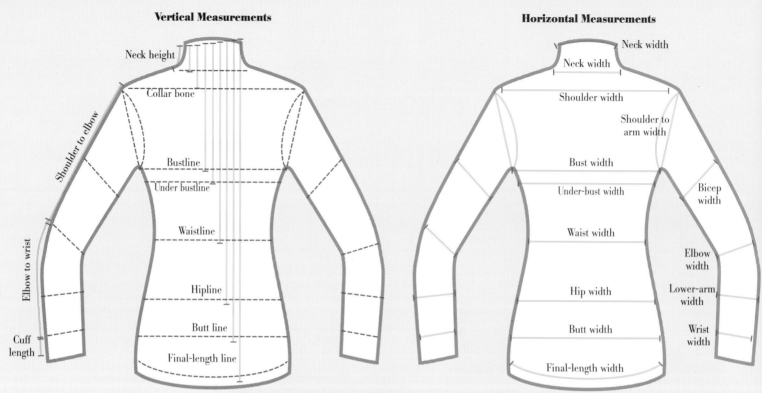

Vertical Measurements

Neck height
Collar bone
Shoulder to elbow
Bustline
Under bustline
Waistline
Elbow to wrist
Hipline
Butt line
Cuff length
Final-length line

Horizontal Measurements

Neck width
Neck width
Shoulder width
Shoulder to arm width
Bust width
Under-bust width
Bicep width
Waist width
Elbow width
Hip width
Lower-arm width
Butt width
Wrist width
Final-length width

Making a pattern template

This pattern fits a size medium with a shrink factor (SF) of about 1.3 for a medium- to heavy-weight coat. If you want a lighter-weight coat, the SF would be closer to 1.45 and the size would also be closer to a small.

These are instructions on how to make a basic template for a jacket/coat. You can make all kinds of modifications to these patterns, from shortening the length, adding longer arms, taking out the coat collar, or adding a taller collar to taking off the sleeves to make a vest. This coat pattern has a bit of a flare at the bottom. It is fitted yet has room for thicker underclothing.

Horizontal Measurements (in inches) Coat, Size Medium, Shrink Factor 1.3	Body Measurement / Final Garment Measurement	Template Measurement (Body Measurement ÷ 2) × Shrink Factor
Neck circumference (at top of garment)	16.5	10.75
Neck circumference (at collarbone)	17.75	11.5
Shoulder circumference	41.5	27
Shoulder-to-armpit circumference	20.75	13.5
Bicep circumference	13.8	9
Elbow circumference	13	8.5
Lower-arm circumference	11.5	7.5
Wrist circumference	10.75	7
Bust circumference (at nipple line)	40	26
Under-bust circumference	38	25
Waist circumference	37	24
Hip circumference	38	25
Butt circumference	43	28
Circumference at base of garment	50.75	32

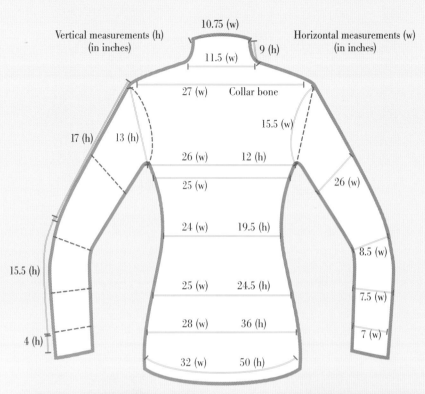

The arm has a slight bend at the elbow to create a natural fit.

The tables overleaf show the body measurements used and the template measurements (accounting for the formula and shrink factor).
To start, create a small sketch of the pattern with the horizontal and vertical measurements before you go large scale. Begin mapping out the vertical points, then add the corresponding horizontal measurements. Left is a template sketch labeling the measurements for the coat.

Make a copy of this sketch and fill in your own measurements.

Vertical Measurements (in inches) Coat, Size Medium, Shrink Factor 1.3	Body Measurement Inches / cm	Template Measurement (Body Measurement × Shrink Factor) Inches / cm
Neck height (measured from collarbone)	7 / 18	9 / 23
Collarbone to bust/nipple line	9 / 23	12 / 30
Collarbone to under bustline	11 / 28	14.5 / 37
Collarbone to waistline	15 / 38	19.5 / 50
Collarbone to hipline	18.75 / 48	24.5 / 62
Collarbone to buttocks line	27.75 / 70	36 / 91
End of shoulder to armpit	10 / 25	13 / 33
End of shoulder to elbow	13 / 33	17 / 43
Elbow to wrist (allow extra inches for a cuff if desired)	12 (15) / 30 (38)	15.5 (19.5 with cuff) / 39 (50)
Collarbone to final length of garment	35.5 / 90	46 / 117

Next, transfer your drawing to a larger scale. Using heavy 6 mm painters' plastic, start mapping out the vertical points first with tick marks, using a smudge-proof marker. For the corresponding horizontal measurements, the horizontal point should match up with the vertical point halfway through. When all the tick marks are made, connect them together with the marker. Fold the pattern in half horizontally along the vertical tick marks. Make sure that both sides match up, and make any necessary adjustments before you cut the pattern out.

For the coat pattern, because there are more-complex lines to draw for the arm, start by drawing a torso and then one arm. You can draw half of the pattern first; fold it along the vertical axis and draw out the other side by tracing the marker you can see through the pattern. Make sure both sides match up, and then cut out the pattern.

Remove all the marker lines with rubbing alcohol before you use the pattern, since they can rub off onto your garment when it is soapy and wet.

The beauty of nuno felting is that it is forgiving, flexible, and intuitive. Starting with the basic principles mentioned in this section, you can play with your designs and patterns and have predictable results. For each design, have a good plan and execution strategy of how you want your designs to look in the end; however, leave room for play, modifications, and discovery.

How much wool to use in the project

To estimate how much wool you will need in your project, you can weigh your sample piece and measure the surface area of your final sample, then estimate the surface area of both sides of your project pattern and input the numbers into the formula below.

(Sample weight × final pattern surface area) ÷ surface area of sample = amount of wool needed.

This formula and method work to find the amount of wool you need for the project; however, it is tricky to measure the surface area since it is not a simple square shape.

Another method is to use your own experiments and experience for estimating how much wool you need. For example, my jackets and coats (depending on length) need around 1.5–3 lbs. of wool. For an airy tunic, I use somewhere around 16–18 oz. of wool. You can weigh your projects after they are complete, and make notes for future reference.

As long as your final pattern layout reflects the thickness of wool in your sample, you can calculate a good estimate of how much wool you need.

However, it's sensible to have more than enough wool for a project in case you want to add design elements or change the pattern around. Take reference photos of the sample layout if necessary. You can also save sample layout strands of wool as a reference for the final layout.

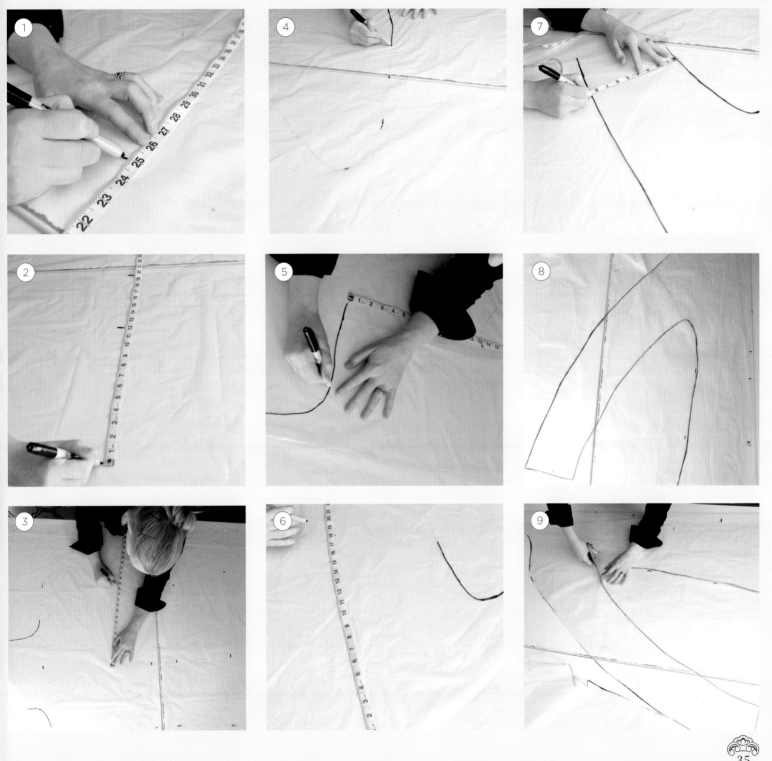

Tips for Longevity and Design Success

Over my years of felting, I have come up with a number of useful pointers for designing and creating success. They have been good guidelines for me in my felt work, and I hope you find them useful too.

Practical Felting Tips

- **Good posture!** The better your posture, the longer you will be able to felt, and the less pain you will feel. I felt in front of a mirror so I can routinely check my posture. The mirror also helps me see different perspectives of my work, which can be really useful.
- **Take routine breaks and stretches.** If you get stiff or sore, stretch your arms, back, and legs. If you are hitting a wall with a project, go grab a snack or cup of tea. You will feel refreshed when you come back to your work. Sometimes, I need several days or even weeks away from certain projects. I am amazed at how differently I see the challenges after a mental and physical rest.
- **Establish a correct felt table height!** I cannot stress this enough. If you need to get table risers or have a felt table custom-made to fit your height, this will help protect your back from strain. My table comes to about my hip bone. Any lower, and I immediately feel the strain on my back. I can go a little bit higher; however, too much higher limits my reach across the table and therefore my efficiency.
- **Use padded standing mats.** These can be very helpful; they absorb pressure from your joints and will make eight-hour standing days a lot more tolerable.
- **Stay hydrated and fueled with healthy food.** Felting is a physically demanding exercise, so you will require plenty of water and routine snack breaks.
- **Wear comfortable clothing and shoes.** Flat, supportive running shoes with padded soles are my best friends when felting. I like breathable, comfortable clothes that are tighter fitting. Avoid loose-fitting, drapey clothing, since it can drag over your felting projects.
- **Full and stretch your felt well.** To make strong felt that can withstand wear and abrasion, full your fibers to completion. This is done by agitating the fibers in the fulling process, and also stretching your fibers in between the fulling until your felt is strong and tight and no longer has loose fibers.

When you press the fibers between your fingers, they should feel tight and dense—not squishy. Fibers that are not fulled completely can come undone and pill easily.

- **Be consistent in your layouts.** Make sure the fibers are evenly laid out in each place on your project to keep consistency in your shrinking. Be patient, take your time, and observe how you lay out your wool.
- **Make a sample before you begin a project.** This will quickly help you test the wool layout, shrinkage, and design before you invest in a larger piece and more materials. When I start a new felting idea or collection, I like to do a selection of samples to compare—which weight, colors, patterns, and layout I like best. I also make color dye swatches of nuno felt and include the dye recipes for each color. Keep your samples in a binder for future reference.
- **Organize your materials.** Make sure you have everything you need in the right place before you start your project. If you buy your materials in bulk, not only will it be cheaper, it will prevent you from running out of materials at a critical design/creation moment.
- **Connect with a felting community.** Whether online or in person, find

your felting tribe that you can bounce ideas off and share ideas with, and who can support you in your felting journey. There is a lot of good to be found in uniting with others who share your passion.

- **Find a felting instructor.** I've read a lot of books on felting that were helpful, and watched tutorial videos. However, big improvements in my felting have come from taking workshops from felt instructors with innovative and advanced felting techniques. There are so many types of felting with a reservoir of information to discover and apply to your own work. You can ask questions and problem-solve with an instructor and other students at a workshop. Almost every advanced felter I know takes workshops from other felters for their own discovery and growth. A felt instructor is absolutely worth the investment!

Anita Larkin, felt instructor, and Jenny Hill at the 2015 Felter's Fling in Massachusetts.

Design Tips

- **Have a well-thought-out and drafted plan.** Before starting designs, it is good practice to begin with a rough or detailed sketch to give you a good idea of the direction of the project. This limits wasted time and frustration in achieving your desired final outcome.
- **Keep track of your inspiration.** I recommend that you use a sketchbook/journal or (physical or digital) inspiration board. Sketch out your designs, keep magazine clippings, and include fabric swatches and notes on your projects for reference. You never want to forget a great design idea. You can bring your sketchbook along with you on vacation, walks, etc., to capture any inspiration that comes to you. It's good to sketch all kinds of things, from details for a dress to the curves and lines for silhouettes.
- **Don't wait for the perfect plan to execute.** Having a general idea of what you want to do is important, but sometimes it's too easy to procrastinate before starting a project. Maybe we are afraid of ruining expensive fibers or fabrics we bought. Truly, the fibers and materials are much better felted into a piece than sitting on the shelf. It's important to experiment and take risks. We learn and grow only by doing. Be brave!
- **Be authentic in your creations.** Create what you are most excited about. You may be inspired by others' work from time to time, but always make your designs your own work. I get inspiration from all around me—anything and everything from current and past fashion trends to nature. Most of my inspiration comes when I travel and absorb the colors and flavors of a new culture and landscape. I find if a creation comes from my heart and mind, it is usually well received.
- **Think carefully when choosing colors.** Color is very important in all forms of art. It gives a mood and vibe to each piece. In my work, I like to use complementary colors, neutrals, monochromes, and bold pops of color. I strive to find balance in my colors and for them to make sense in the context of my design—to add to the overall aesthetic, not to distract from it. For color inspiration, reference the annual *Pantone Fashion Color Report*, which gives forecasts into color popularity and seasonal trends. Pantone also illustrates great use of color in fashion and design. I find great color combinations by doing an internet images search, using the keywords "color palettes." Nature is another great source of inspiration for color.
- **Have fun!** This should go without saying. However, if I ever find myself creating something that doesn't make me happy, I realize it's time to change things up and start afresh.

GUIDED PROJECTS

A beautiful lightweight
and structured nuno felt
scarf with fringe tassels,
made using various
neutral shades of wool.

Marbled Scarf with Fringe

What you will learn:

With this project you will blend fibers and create a marbled texture with defining lines.

- Basic wool layout, layering, and nuno felt techniques
- How to create a marbled design with wool and other blending techniques
- How to calculate shrinkage of layout and fulling
- How to create tassels at the ends of the scarf

Material List:

- 4–8 oz. of 19-micron merino wool in various neutral or monotone colors: gray, black, charcoal, and white
- 92 × 13 in., 4.5 mm silk gauze, undyed or dyed your color of choice
- Basic felt tools: see pages 16–21
- Two 15 × 12 in. sheets of plastic for resist layers (about the weight of a garbage bag)
- Optional: uncarded raw fibers such as mohair or silk (or both) roving for extra shine and texture

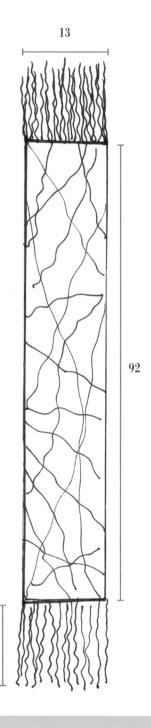

13

92

11

Final width and length (without tassels): 10 in. wide × 70 in. long
(The final width before trimming the scarf edges was 10 in., so I will
use the width measurement before trimming in the formula).
Final tassel length (from scarf edge): 9 in. per side

Shrink Factor:
Horizontal SF (width): 1.3 SF
Vertical SF (length): 1.3 SF

Horizontal SF
10 in. × (SF) = 13 in. → 13 in. / 10 in. = 1.3 SF
Vertical SF:
70 in. × (SF) = 92 in. → 92 in. / 70 in. = 1.3 SF

├────────┤ **Measurements in Inches**

Inch / Centimeter
Conversion
13 / 43
11 / 36
92 / 234

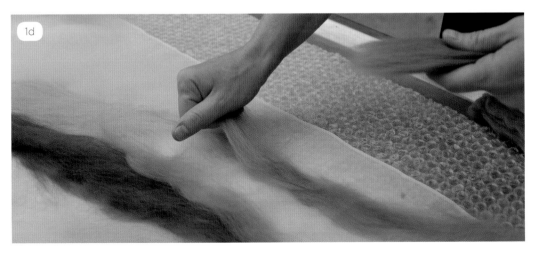

1) Lay the silk piece flat onto the bubble mat. If there are wrinkles in the silk, sprinkle water over the top and smooth out the piece. Start out laying light blocks of colored wool that slightly overlap on the silk piece. [1c]

To test the thickness of your roving layer: hold it up to your eye; it should mostly obscure your vision, but you should also be able to see through it. [1a]

Each piece laid should overlap half of the next piece (see page 23). To keep the layout smooth, if you are right handed, lay left to right; conversely, if you are left handed, lay right to left. [1b]

If you see any holes or light spots that show the silk piece through your layout, lay dust layers of roving over the top. A dust layer is half to a quarter as thick as the base roving layer. It is important to keep the layout thickness consistent, so dust layers should even out the layers and not make some patches thicker.

In each of your chosen shades, lay blocks of color out in wavy lines, slightly overlapping each color to ensure there are no gaps in the layout. Allow your wool layout to hang off the silk piece edge by about 1/4 in. [1d]

2) After the solid blocks of color completely cover the silk, blend the blocks of color together with light, wispy layers of roving. This is the decorative layer, so keep the roving very light.

With each color, take a 24 in. long piece of roving. From top to bottom, split each strand into four or six thinner strands, varying in width. Hold the end tip of a strand and lightly pull the strand along, guiding the wool into a thin, wispy layer between each block of color. This will blend the contour lines and soften the edges along the blocks of wool. [2a]

Pull off wispy layers of wool and create dust layers on top of contrasting colors. For example, spread wispy white wool over the top of charcoal wool to create a pop effect. [2b]

3) Evaluate your design by standing back—even getting on a chair for a bird's-eye view of your project—to see where colors need to be balanced or added. When you are happy with the blocks of color and blended tones, start to dry-felt the wool and silk together.

Lightly place your hands for a few seconds over each section of wool, softly yet firmly vibrating your hands in small up-and-down motions. Each up-and-down motion should not exceed more than 1/2 in. of space. [3a] The dry-felting will lightly bond the wool and silk together and prepare you for the next fulling stages. [3b]

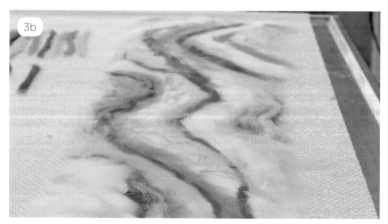

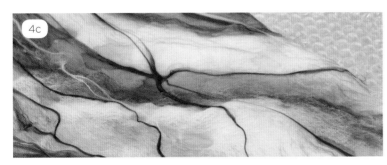

4) Add some defining lines to your scarf design. Peel off thin strands of roving about 1–3 ft. in length and ¹⁄₈ in. wide. Sprinkle some water on the bubble mat and lightly roll the strands in the water to fully saturate the fibers so they stick together. [4a]

Start placing the wet wool strands on top of your felt design. Go in between blocks of color and create interesting patterns over the top. These wool lines will stay defined, while the bottom wool layers will blend together. [4b]

Put contrasting colored lines over solid blocks of color. At this stage take another elevated view of your project to see where you need more lines, or where you need to adjust them. [4c]

5) Create tassels for the end of the scarf by peeling off fifty strands of roving, approximately 11 in. long (twenty-five strands for each side). The width of each strand should be about ½ in. There can be some variation in length and width. Use the same colors of roving as used in the scarf, and use the same amount of each tassel color. [5a]

Sprinkle water on the mat and rub soap on top of the water. Roll each tassel strand in the soapy water until it firms up a little. Leave 1½ in. of the tassel dry and unfelted. The dry portion will be used to attach to the scarf. The width and length after you rub the tassel should be the way you want them on the finished scarf. You can vary your tassel thickness if you are not happy with the width and length. [5b]

After you full each tassel, prepare both ends of the scarf for the tassel attachment. Dry-felt each end of the scarf and tuck the overhanging fiber strands under the silk base. You want a smooth edge on the scarf before you attach the tassels. [5c]

Place twenty-five tassels on each side of the scarf, in alternating colors. [5d] Attach only the dry portion to the edge of the scarf. Take each dry end of the strand and lightly pull the wool to thin out the strand and blend the wool into the scarf. [5e] Place a dust layer of wool over top of the tassel strands in the same direction as they were laid out.

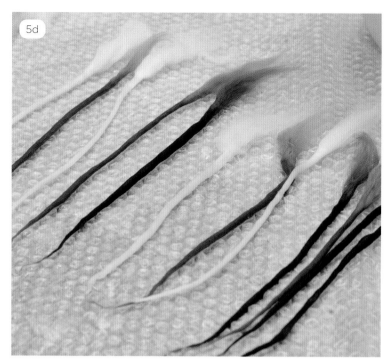

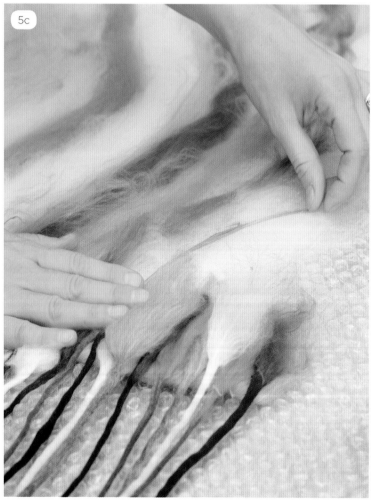

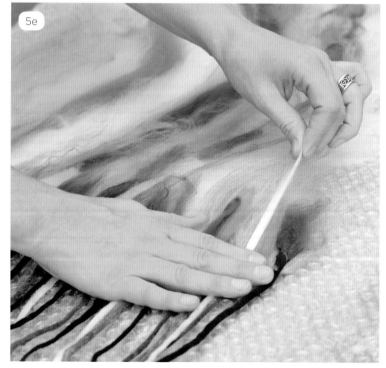

6) Lightly disperse water over the top of the project. As there are many layers of wool that you do not want disturbed, it is best to start out watering with a garden pump sprayer on a low pressure setting and gradually build up to more water pressure. Hold the water nozzle at a 90° angle to prevent moving the wool around. [6] I always wet the surface before I cover it with netting. This prevents the wool from sticking to the netting and lets the wool fibers come together faster.

7) Tuck the edges of wool hanging off the sides under the base layer of silk. Seal and smooth out the edges with your fingers. You may want to put soap on your fingers to create a lubricant while smoothing the fibers down. [7a]

Make sure the fibers are folded right under at the silk edge and that the entire scarf edge is straight and smooth. Sealing the fiber edges is very important for the end product to look clean and refined. [7b]

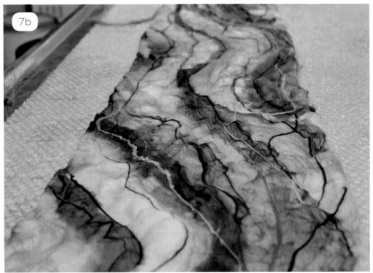

8) Cover the layout with the open-weave plastic netting. Rub or dispense soap on top of the netting, allowing the soap to seep through to the layout underneath. [8a–b]

Start agitating the surface with a hand-felting tool such as a palm washboard. Begin by rubbing the edges and the connecting points of the tassels in the direction of the layout. Work your way into the center of the design and then switch to circular and perpendicular rubbing motions. [8c]

After about five or ten minutes of rubbing, lightly remove the netting. Hold the felt project with one hand while you lightly jiggle the netting off with the other hand, to prevent uprooting any part of the design that is stuck to the netting. Check the project for any underagitated areas to focus on in the final rubdown.

Place the netting on one more time and rub the surface for a final five minutes, or however long you need to seal down the fibers and connect them to the silk base.

9) Remove the netting. Place a resist layer of plastic at the edge of the scarf, where the tassels begin. Flip each tassel over the edge of the plastic, avoiding any overlap with other tassels. The plastic resist layer will prevent the tassels from felting onto the project. (Note: If your bubble mat is long enough, you will not need to do this folding-over step; otherwise, fold as necessary.) [9a]

Take a plastic rolling rod and roll the bubble mat and project around the rod in the direction the project was laid out. Keep the mat tight when rolling it up. Secure the roll with bubble mat ties. Tie in a bow so it can easily be untied at the end of the rolling. Drain out any excess water by tipping the roll over the top of a bucket. Roll the mat up in a dry towel to absorb moisture. [9b]

Roll the project five hundred times: each roll count is from your palms to your elbows and back to your palms. This takes approximately seven to ten minutes, depending on how long it takes you to roll. You may want to set a timer when you begin, so you don't lose track.

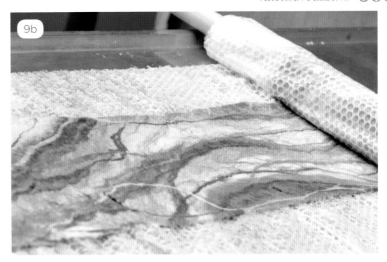

10) Unroll the mat. Begin the fulling process by rubbing the silk side of your design against the bubble mat in the direction of the layout, and then perpendicular to the direction of the layout. [10a–b] When you see the silk starting to crinkle up, flip the project and rub the wool side in the same directions on the bubble mat.

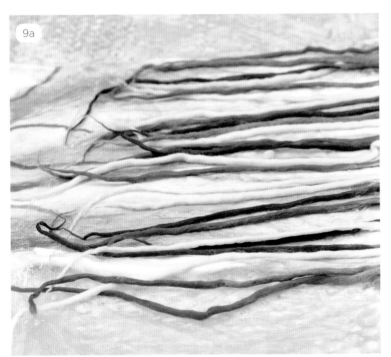

11) Ball the scarf up and knead it one hundred times. [11a]

Stretch the scarf in vertical and horizontal directions to smooth out the felt texture. [11b] Continue rubbing the scarf both vertically and horizontally on the bubble mat until you feel it firm up. Feel and look at the surface for any loose fibers. [11c]

Rub the tassels against the bubble mat until they are very firm. The project should feel firm and not squishy before you are ready to wash out the soap. [11d]

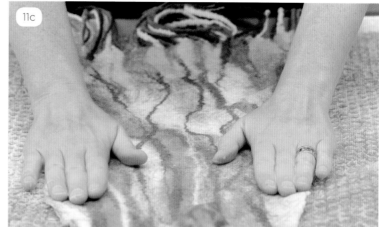

12) Using room-temperature water, rinse out all the soap from the scarf. When you squeeze the project, you should not see any soap suds. Then place the scarf in a spin dryer to extract the water. [12]

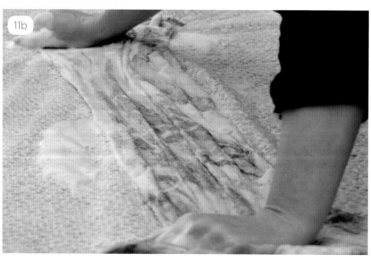

13) Final shaping: stretch the areas needed, including the tassels. I can get several more inches on each side of a project by doing this final stretch. [13a]

If you want a straighter edge, trim off any curves. [13b] After you cut the edge, be sure to seal the fibers up by rubbing the edge in a perpendicular direction against a wet and soapy area on your bubble mat. Be sure to rinse that section out again with water.

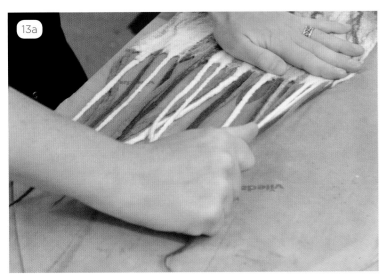

14) Iron the project to give a crisp look to the surface, and flatten out any waves in the scarf. [14a] Place over a mannequin or rod to dry. If you want to shape the scarf so that it curves around the shoulders and neck, you can use the curves of the mannequin. [14b] Do your final measurements while the scarf is on the mannequin, and any last stretching or shaping. [14c]

This modern, eclectic poncho fits small to large sizes depending on how you like the fit. (There's a larger-sized variation too). It features a bold 3-D geometric pattern surface texture and is created with wool at the base and silk on the outside.

3-D Textured Poncho

What you will learn:

This poncho uses an intermediate technique of creating seams with a felt pattern, using a plastic resist.

- How to create 3-D texture with felt
- How to use a poncho felt pattern
- How to make felt seams
- How to shape structured necklines and arms

Material List:

- 16 oz. of 19-micron merino wool in various neutral or monotone colors: gray, black, charcoal, white (I used about 8 oz. of white, 4 oz. of black, and 4 oz. of dark-gray merino wool)
- 2½ yds. of 4.5 mm undyed silk gauze
- Basic felt tools: (see pages 16–21)

- 54 × 42 in. sheet of resist pattern plastic* for the poncho pattern (*I recommend using 6 mm painters' plastic for resist material)
- 20 × 50 in. sheet of resist plastic, lighter weight (about the weight of a garbage bag)

For 3-D Texture

Two sheets of fully felted, medium-weight nuno felt (silk base, wool top layer) approximately 30 × 20 in., cut into forty strips ranging from 2–30 in. long by ½–¾ in. wide. One piece of white, and one gray, from the same-colored roving used in the project. The thickness of the prefelted pieces should be about the same thickness as the final poncho. I save a lot of scrap pieces of felt that I recycle for just such purposes.

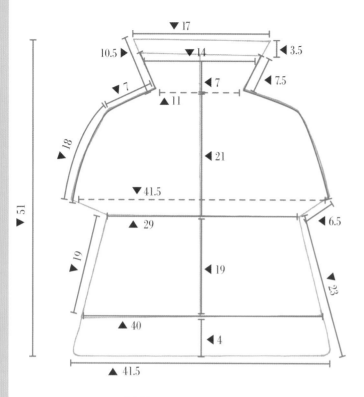

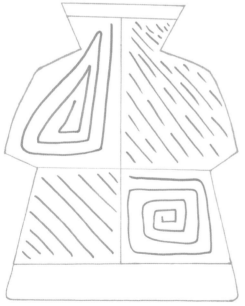

Final Width and Length
Width: 27 in. (arm to arm)
Length: 30 in. (top of collar to base)

Pattern Width and Length
Width : 41.5 in. (arm to arm)
Length: 47 in. (top of collar to base)

Shrink Factor:
Horizontal SF (width): 1.53
Vertical SF (length): 1.56

Horizontal Shrink Factor:
27 in. × (SF): 41.5 in. ➙ 41.5 in. / 27 in.: 1.53 SF

Vertical Shrink Factor:
30 in. × (SF): 47 in. ➙ 47 in. / 30 in.: 1.56 SF

Note: The vertical shrink factor is slightly larger because the collar was fulled longer than the rest of the poncho. Using an estimated 1.5 SF for this project will be sufficient.

	Seam
	Measurements in Inches

Inch / Centimeter conversion	
17 / 43	41.5 / 105
14 / 36	6.5 / 16
3.5 / 89	29 / 74
10.5 / 27	19 / 48
7.5 / 19	23 / 58
7 / 18	40 / 101
11.5 / 29	4 / 10
18 / 46	47 / 119
21 / 53	

1) Create your poncho pattern out of the resist pattern plastic. I made this pattern 4 in. longer at the base, and 3½ in. taller at the collar, to allow you to modify your pattern for this or future projects. See a sketch of the pattern on page 54, including the dimensions for the layout used in the project, plus additional inches for project modifications (see pages 30–35, "Pattern Template Creation").

The pattern for this poncho fits sizes small to large, depending on how you like the fit. This project has about a 1.5 shrink factor. If you are looking for a large to extra-large fit, extend your layout to the bottom edge of the pattern—an additional 4 in. in the layout. Also, if you want a taller, more exaggerated collar, extend the layout 2–3½ in. on the collar layout to the edge of the pattern.

2) The layout design for this pattern consists of four rectangle shapes divided on each side of the garment, as shown in the pattern sketch. Start by marking your pattern in quarters with a heavy pencil or tape.

Find the midway points at the top of the collar, the neckline, and the base of the poncho. Draw a vertical line from the top point through the neckline midpoint to the bottom point. Next, draw a horizontal line at the base of where the poncho arms end. These lines will break up each quadrant of your design and act as a guide for laying out each section.

Place the pattern on a large sheet of bubble mat in the direction that fits your felt table. If your table width is under 42 in., you will have to shift your pattern around the table in the layout phase and work in sections. [2]

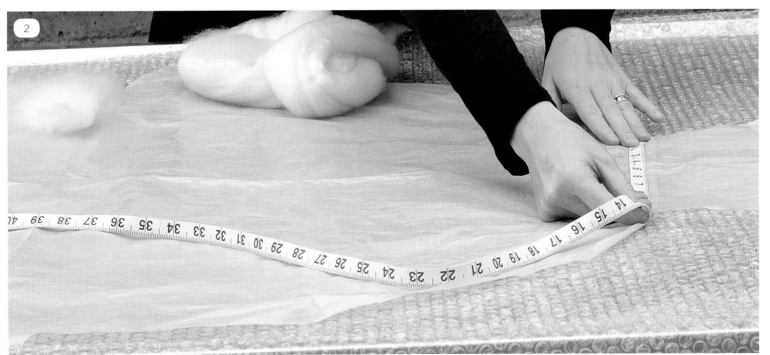

3) Lay out the back side of the poncho. Start by laying out the bottom left quadrant in white merino wool. The width of the rectangle shape should be about 20 in. wide by 19 in. tall (and 4 in. from the pattern base, unless you are extending the layout size). [3]

Lay an outline of the rectangle shape to create defined lines within the sectioned-off lines you've already marked. Lay medium-weight wool on the left side of the quadrant, just at the edge of the pattern, and do not allow the fibers to extend past the pattern, since this portion will become an edge, not a seam (see page 23, "Wool Layout"). [3]

Continue laying this block of color by filling in the section in an up-and-down direction. Fill in any gaps or weak spots of the layout with dust layers of wool. Keep the wool weight consistent. Smooth out the edges of the rectangle layout to keep them looking straight.

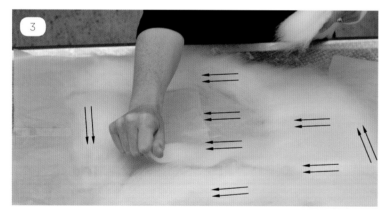

4) Move on to the top left quadrant and lay out the dark-gray wool in this divided section. Begin laying the wool at the top of the collar, which starts 3.5 in. below the top of the pattern (unless you plan to extend the collar layout for a larger, more dramatic collar). [4a]

Lay the wool perpendicular to the pattern, with 1½ in. of wool coming off the pattern edge. The overhang of fibers will later flip over the edge of the pattern to create a seam. [4b]

At the arm line and neckline, do not extend the wool past the edge of the pattern, since this will be an armhole, not a seam. Create an outline with the gray wool and slightly overlap the gray wool on top of the white wool below by ¼ in. It is important to create the overlap so the sections fuse and become seamless, without any holes in the layout.

Continue to fill in the shape with an up-and-down directional layout.

Make sure the right edge of the gray wool lines up vertically with the white wool below. Look for weak spots and holes in the wool layout

and cover with dust layers of fiber, keeping the layout consistent. [4c]

5) Next, work on the top right quadrant, using the white wool. Start laying wool out as in step 4, only the other way round (i.e., mirror imaged). [5a]

Overlap the white wool over the gray layer by ¼ in. Smooth and straighten out the edge. [5b]

6) Complete the last quadrant on the bottom right with black wool as in step 3, only mirror imaged. [6a]

Overlap the wool on the bottom left quadrant and top right quadrant by ¼ in., as in steps 4 and 5. [6b]

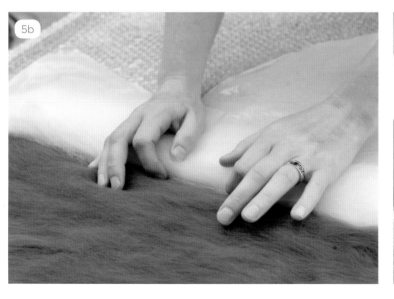

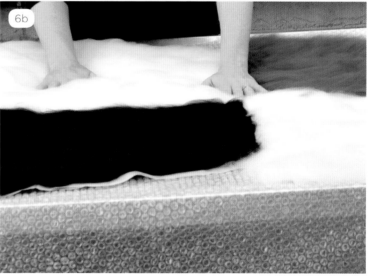

7) After each quadrant is laid out and the pattern lines look smooth, begin to dry-felt the wool by gently placing your hands on the layout and lightly vibrating your hands in an up-and-down motion. [7a]

The connection points of the quadrants are especially important, so make sure each section fuses together. [7b]

Look and feel for thin layers of wool and place dust layers over the top to even out any inconsistency. [7c]

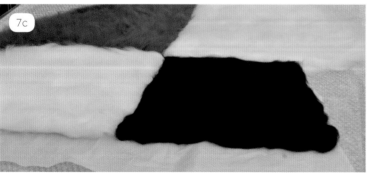

8) Using the same roving as on the poncho, create four felt ropes each 120 in. long. Make two black ropes and two gray ropes. Split off ½ in. wide strips of roving. You can mix colors together, such as white with gray, so long as you keep the width to about ½ in. [8a]

Lay each roving strip on top of a dry bubble mat surface and roll each piece gently like a strip of dough, with your hands rolling in a perpendicular direction to the wool. [8b]

When the wool starts to join together, sprinkle some water and add a little soap to the surface of the bubble mat, next to the wool strands. Begin rolling the felt cords in the water and soap until they become solid. Add more water or soap as needed.

To avoid working with really long strands of wool, you can create several shorter rope strands and tie them together to get a total of 120 in. per rope.

9) Take one black and one gray rope strand and create a spiral shape in the white sections. Start with the outside of the spiral and work your way to the center. [9a]

Make your spiral similar to the shape of the section you are laying in. Allow ¾ in. of space between the edge of the layout and the spiral, and also between each spiral strand. Keep in mind that the spacing between each spiral strand will shrink when felted. [9b–c]

Continue laying the next spiral on the top right white section. [9d-f]

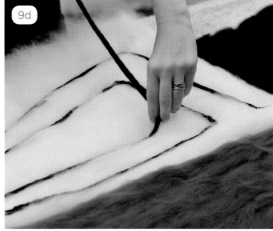

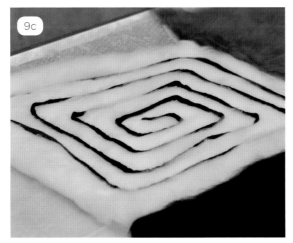

10) Cut the prefelted pieces into strips ranging between 2 and 30 in. long by ½–¾ in. wide. There should be around forty white strips and twenty gray strips. [10a]

Place the gray strips on top of the black section in a diagonal pattern. Allow for 1–1½ in. spacing between each strip. [10b]

Use the white strips to do another diagonal pattern with the same amount of spacing on the top left gray quadrant. Allow for 2 in. of space between the edge of the diagonal strips and the edge of the layout. [10c]

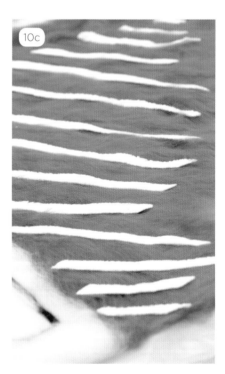

11) Assess your layout. [11a] If you are happy with it, place a sheet of silk gauze over the top of the design. [11b] This silk will felt to all of the wool layers underneath and keep the 3-D patterns intact.

Cut along the edge of the silk so it lines up with the wool layout underneath. [11c] Allow for a ½ in. overhang of silk over the wool layout. [11d]

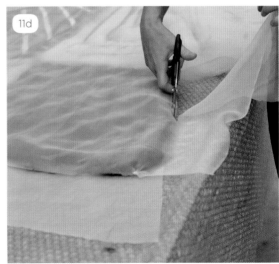

12) Wet down the entire layout. Saturate it fully but avoid puddles of water. Make sure there is enough saturation on top of the spirals and felt diagonals, since more water will be required in these areas to fully saturate the pieces.

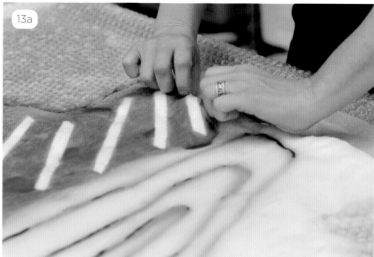

13) Tuck and seal the silk edge underneath the wool at the edges of the layout—such as the neckline, arm edges, left and right bottom sides, and base edge of the layout. Do not seal the edges on the portions that will become seams. [13a–b]

14) Cover the project with felt netting.
Rub or disperse soap over the top of the netting, allowing the soap to seep through onto the project. [14a–b]

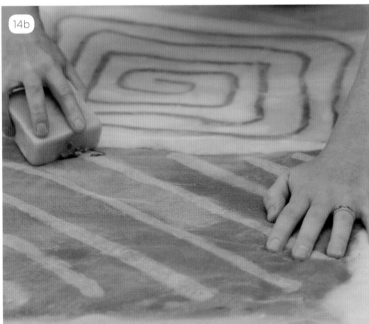

15) Use a hand-felting tool to gently agitate the layout. Start at the edges and work your way into the center of the piece.

Make sure to gently and thoroughly rub in between the spirals and diagonal strips to ensure the silk fuses to the wool underneath, and that the objects don't shift while rubbing. [15a]

When the layout feels like it has come together and compressed down well, lightly jiggle the felt netting off the layout. [15b]

16) Look to see which areas need more rubbing—especially for places where the silk is not fully attached onto the wool layout. For this, use a palm-sized piece of bubble mat and rub the bubbles against the project, especially between the rope layers. [16]

Place the felt netting over the project and rub down one last time, being sure to go over the areas that need more agitation. Remove the felt netting after your last pass with the hand-felting tool.

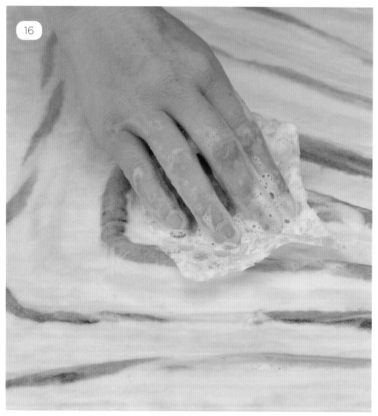

17) At the corner where the neckline and shoulder meet, cut small slits into the piece at 45° angles, stopping the slit ¼ in. before the pattern edge. [17a]

Flip the shoulder, arm, and neck seams onto the other side of the pattern. Crease and seal down the edges at the arms, sides, neckline, and base of the pattern. [17b–c]

18) Flip the pattern by grabbing the top and bottom sides of the project. Smooth out the pattern after you flip it. [18a]

Open up the seams. (We originally flipped the seams over to allow the layout to stick to the pattern when it was flipped over.) [18b]

Begin laying white wool in the top left quadrant. Lay the wool at the edge of the pattern half as thick as elsewhere, since you will flip the seam back over and you don't want the seam to be too thick. On this side, do not lay wool off the edge of the pattern, since you have already created your seams. Lay the rest of the wool exactly as it was laid on the other side of the pattern. The layout should line up with the white layout underneath the pattern. [18c]

On the right-side edge of this top left quadrant, add an additional 2½ in. wide layer of wool to create an overlap for the front panels. Curve the layout at the top of the collar. [18d]

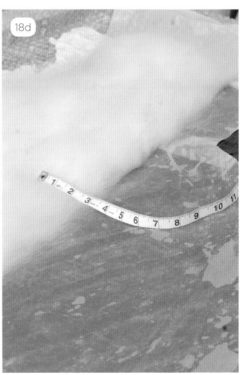

19) When you have finished laying the white wool, flip over the left-side seam from the neck and shoulder to the arm. [19a] Pull the edges firmly and gently over the pattern edge so it butts right up against the plastic. [19b]

Gently pat the seam down. Lay a dust layer of wool over the top of the seam and new layer. [19c]

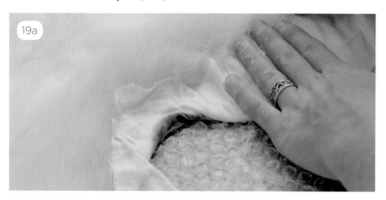

20) Next, lay out the bottom left black quadrant. Slightly overlap the black wool onto the white wool by ¼ in. Add an extra 2½ in. to the right side of the panel, making sure it lines up with the above white quadrant edge. [20]

Dry-felt the white and black sections.

21) Add a spiral shape on the white wool with the remaining gray felt rope, in the same way as laid on the back side of the pattern.

Lay the remaining white, cut-up, prefelted pieces in a diagonal pattern on the black section. [21]

22) Cover the panel with silk gauze. Cut the silk along the edges of the wool layout. Leave a ½ in. overhang on the edges. [22a–b]

At the seams, make sure the silk touches the edge of the silk that was flipped over.

23) Saturate the panel with water as before in step 12.

Tuck the silk under the edges of wool, as described in step 13.

As in steps 14–16, cover with felt netting and disperse soap on top of the layout. Rub the panel down with a hand-felting tool. Start by rubbing the felt seam first. It is important to create a strong seam on the neckline, on the shoulder, and down to the armhole.

Next, focus on rubbing the edges, and work your way into the middle of the layout. As on the other side, be sure to thoroughly and gently rub the 3-D objects and the spaces in between to make sure the silk properly felts to the wool, and that the objects don't shift. [23]

Carefully remove the netting when the panel fibers feel like they have come together. Assess which areas need more rubbing. Cover and continue rubbing needed areas with the hand-felting tool.

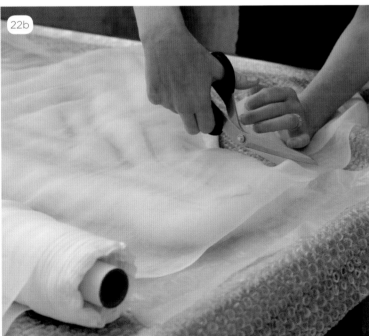

24) Rub the edges of the seams with a small, palm-sized piece of bubble mat, bubble side down. [24] This will smooth down the seam and get rid of bunching. To prevent creating a ridge at the seam, keep the seam as close to the plastic resist as possible.

Smooth and straighten out the neck, armhole, and base edges with your hands.

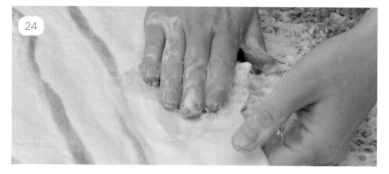

25) Cover the panel with a sheet of thin resist plastic. This will act as a resist between the left panel and the right panel you will lay next. Smooth out the plastic well, getting rid of any wrinkles. [25]

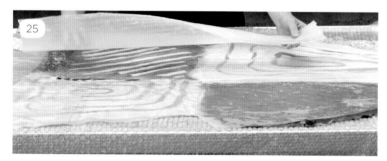

26) Begin the layout for the right panel with the gray wool on the top right quadrant. Lay a light layer on the edge of the seam. Repeat the layout in the same way as with the white wool on the adjacent panel. Be sure to extend the width of this quadrant on the left side by 2½ in. so the panels overlap. [26a]

Flip the right-side seams over onto the gray wool, smoothing them onto the neck, shoulders, and arms. Repeat the process of connecting the seams as in step 19. [26b]

27) Lay out the bottom right quadrant with white wool, using the process described in step 20. Lay the remaining black felt cord onto the bottom right white quadrant. [27]

28) Lay a combination of the remaining gray and white strips onto the top right quadrant, in a diagonal pattern. [28]

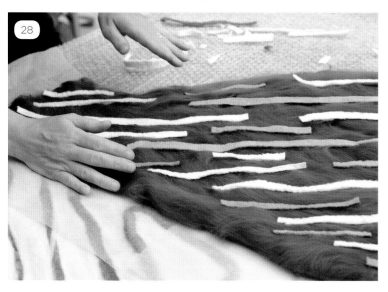

29) Cover the panel with silk and cut out the edges, as described in step 22. [29]

30) For the right panel, follow steps 23–24. [30]

31) Take a plastic rolling rod and roll the bubble mat and project around the rod in the direction the project was laid out. Keep the mat tight when rolling it out. You will notice some bunching as you roll it up—so as you roll, straighten out the fabric by lightly tugging the poncho forward. Secure the roll with bubble mat tie bows, so they can easily be untied at the end of rolling. (See overleaf [31a–b]).

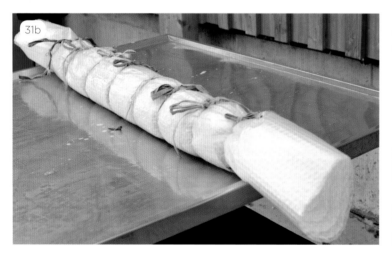

Drain out any excess water by tipping the roll over the top of a bucket. Roll the mat up in a dry towel to absorb moisture.

32) Roll the project a thousand times: each roll count is from your palms to your elbows and back to your palms. This will take fifteen to twenty minutes, depending on how long it takes you to roll. [32]

33) Unroll the mat. Begin the fulling process by rubbing your design against the plastic resist pattern and bubble mat. [33a]

Rub soap on the seams and rub them well against the resist to make sure they are secure and without ridges. It is important to get the

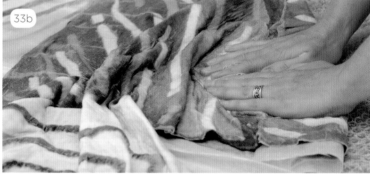

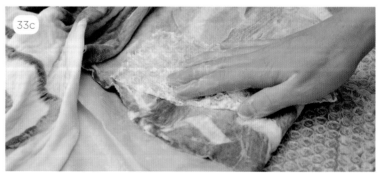

project in a secure place to remove the resist without the seams coming apart. Use the palm-sized sheet of bubble wrap to further seal and smooth the seams. [33b–c]

34) Gently peel the poncho off the plastic resist.

Continue fulling each portion of the poncho, wool side down against the bubble mat. Rub the project in vertical, horizontal, and circular motions against the bubble mat until the poncho starts to feel firm and you can see the silk layer crinkle up from shrinking. [34a]

Flip the poncho over and rub the silk side against the bubbles. In areas where the felt needs more fulling, roll the edges of the poncho

into itself between twenty-five and fifty times. Rub all the edges of the poncho in a perpendicular direction on the bubble mat to firm them up and ensure there are no loose silk pieces. [34b]

35) Ball the poncho up and knead it like bread, a hundred times. [35] Stretch the poncho in vertical and horizontal directions to smooth out the felt texture. Knead a hundred more times. Stretch again.

36) Continue rubbing the poncho in vertical and horizontal directions on the bubble mat until you feel it firm up. [36a] To get a firm neckline that stands on its own while you are wearing the poncho, spend more time fulling the neckline until it feels very firm.

Compare both panel sides to make sure they are even in length and width. Roll and full the poncho in any direction that needs more shrinking or evening out. [36b]

37) Feel and look at both sides of the poncho surfaces for any loose fibers or detached pieces of silk.

Continue rubbing any areas needing more fulling, until they are firm and completely fulled.

The project should feel firm and not squishy before you are ready to wash out the soap. Rinse the soap from the poncho by using room-temperature water, then spin the water out with a spin dryer.

38) Place the damp poncho onto a mannequin. The poncho will have shrunk significantly by this stage, and you can stretch it out several more inches in all directions. Rub the poncho against the mannequin's bust, shoulders, waist, and hips to create a good fit to the body curves. [38a-c]

Use steam to shape the shoulders, arms, neckline, bust, and waist. [38d]

39) Check the final measurements while the poncho is still on the mannequin and do any final stretching or shaping necessary. Let the poncho dry thoroughly on the mannequin.

36a

36b

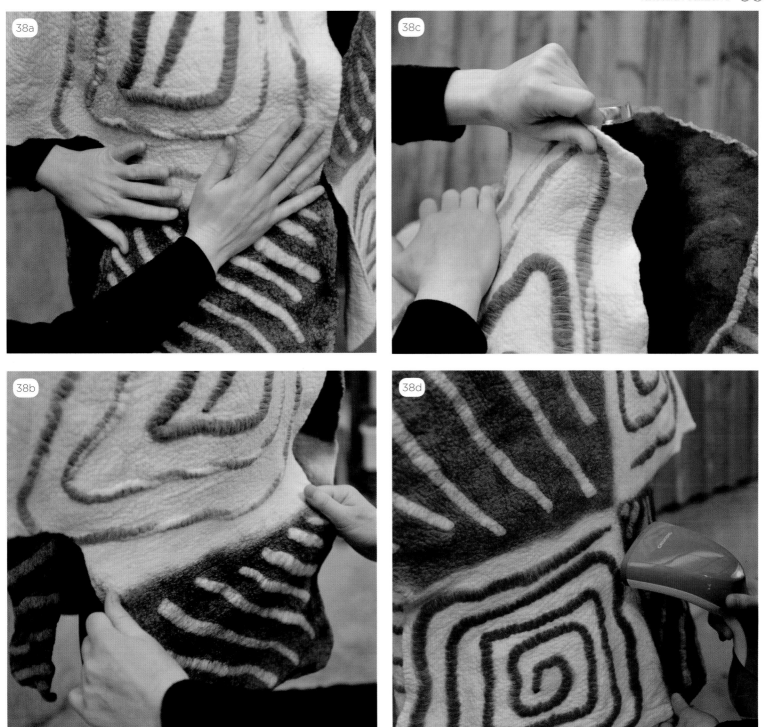

Although this chic vest resembles fur, in common with all other felt projects, it does not require killing any animals to create the textile. Instead it uses rich textures that resemble fur; namely, raw locks, silk roving, yarn, and wool roving. The pattern for this seamless vest fits small to large sizes depending on how you like the fit (there is a larger size variation as well).

Felt Fur Vest

What you will learn:

- How to use intermediate felting techniques and a plastic resist felt pattern
- How to create a luxurious fur texture with various fibers
- How to incorporate various types of fiber into a design
- How to use a vest/tunic felt pattern
- How to shape and fit a vest to the body

Material List:

I used undyed fibers for this entire project to put the emphasis on the natural beauty of the fibers. However, feel free to use a variety of colors in your project.

- 9½ oz. of undyed 19-micron merino wool
- ½ oz. of raw, undyed, unwashed wool locks. I used Wensleydale locks, about 6–8 in. long. Make sure your wool locks are free of vegetable matter, feces, dirt clumps, etc.
- 1½ yds. of 4.5 mm undyed silk gauze
- 2 yds. of textured wool or silk yarn(s). I used two types of wool-textured yarns
- ½ oz. of tussah silk roving
- Basic felt tools: see pages 16-21
- 50 × 32 in. sheet of 6 mm painters' plastic for resist vest pattern
- 15 × 47 in. sheet of resist plastic, lighter weight (about the weight of a garbage bag)

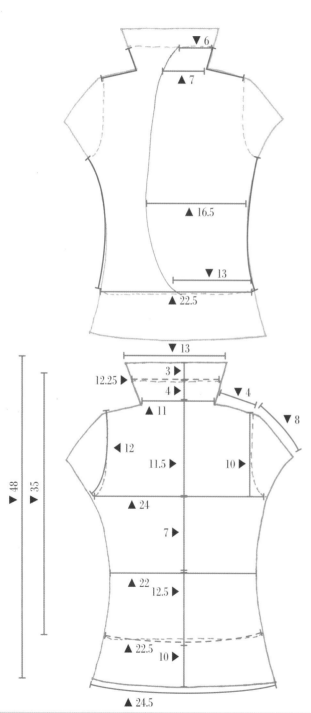

Final Width and Length
Width: 17 in. (vest base)
Length: 25 in. (top of collar to base)

Pattern Width and Length
Width: 22½ in. (vest base)
Length: 35 in. (top of collar to base)

Shrink Factor:
Horizontal SF (width): 1.3
Vertical SF (length): 1.4

Horizontal Shrink Factor
17 in. × (SF): 22½ in. ➝ 22½ in. / 17 in.: 1.3 SF

Vertical Shrink Factor:
25 in. × (SF): 35 in. ➝ 35 in. / 25 in.: 1.4 SF

Note: The vertical shrink factor is slightly larger because the collar was fulled longer than the rest of the vest. Using an estimated 1.4 SF for this project will be sufficient.

├───┤	Seam
├───────┤	Measurements in Inches

Inch / Centimeter conversion

13 / 33	24 / 61
3 / 8	7 / 18
4 / 10	22 / 56
12.25 / 31	12.5 / 32
11 / 28	22.5 / 57
8 / 20	10 / 25
12 / 30	24.5 / 62
10 / 25	35 / 89
11.5 / 29	48 / 121

1) Create your vest pattern out of 6 mm resist pattern plastic. (I used black resist material for this project so the white fibers show up well in the photos. You can use the clear resist material in your pattern.) To allow for longer-vest modifications, I created a pattern size several inches longer than the layout used in this project. Also, I created the pattern with a taller neckline than the layout, and with cap sleeves for additional modification possibilities. See the pattern sketch on page 76 for the dimensions. This project has about 1.4 SF (shrink factor). Make any modifications to the pattern on the basis of your body size and the SF (see pages 30–35).

2) Using the template, begin by laying out the back side of the vest. Lay silk gauze material onto the resist and cut out along your desired pattern edges. When I made this vest, I started my layout 3 in. below the top of the pattern collar and allowed 10 in. from the bottom of the pattern to the bottom of the layout. I suggest you add 2–4 in. to the layout length if you are looking for a longer vest. Additionally, if you want a taller, more exaggerated collar, extend the layout 2–3 in. on the collar layout to the edge of the pattern. At the places on the pattern that will become seams, allow 1½ in. overlay of silk material.

For the edges, cut right in line with where you want the edge to be, such as the bottom edge, neckline, and armholes. [2]

Sprinkle water over the silk so it sticks to the pattern and does not shift when laying wool on top of it.

3) Lay out a medium-weight layer of white wool merino roving directly on top of the silk fabric. Allow a ½ in. overhang of wool on top of the silk material. [3a–b]

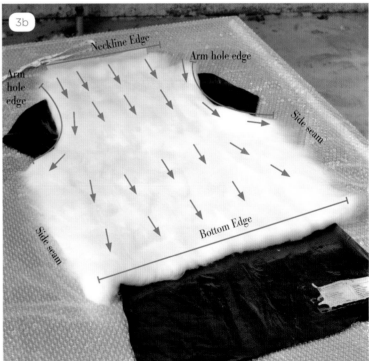

4) Lightly dry-felt the wool roving, to bond the wool fibers to the silk material. Look and feel for weak spots and holes in the layout, and remedy with dust layers of wool. [4a]

Tuck the wool-roving edges under the silk material only at the edges of the pattern (not the seams). [4b]

Dry-felt the tucked-under wool edges. [4c]

5) Take your wool locks and begin placing each one on top of the wool-roving layout. [5a] Keep some locks intact and carefully spread out other locks with your fingers to create a variety in texture. [5b]

Cover the whole layout with locks, allowing some locks to touch. Also allow a ½ in. gap between other locks for additional fibers to be laid out (yarn and silk roving). [5c]

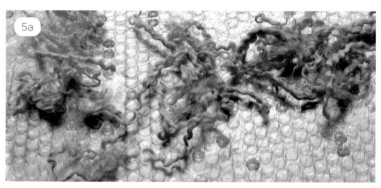

6) Lay out your textured wool yarn in curvy lines between the wool locks. [6]

7) Pull off light strands of tussah silk roving and place in curvy and squiggly lines between the yarn and wool locks. [7a] The silk gives the design a beautiful sheen and texture when felted in. [7b–c]

8) Review the design to see if you are happy with it or need to add additional fibers for balance. [8a]

Carefully saturate the design with water. Hold the water dispenser at a 90° angle to avoid disturbing the fibers. Seal and smooth out the edges of the layout (not the seams). [8b–c]

9) Cover the project with felt netting. Rub or disperse soap over the top of the netting, allowing soap to seep through onto project. [9a–b]

Use a hand-felting tool to gently agitate the layout. Start with the edges and work your way into the center of the piece. [9c]

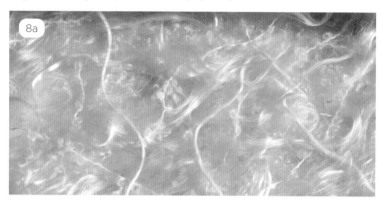

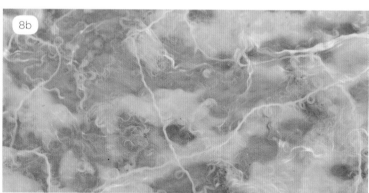

10) After about ten minutes of gentle agitation, carefully remove the felt netting. Hold one hand down on the layout while you lightly jiggle the felt netting off. Since there are many fibers used in this piece, they are likely to stick to the netting, so be very patient and gentle in removing the netting.

Place your hand over any areas where the fibers are coming up and off the silk, and lightly rub them down. [10a] Seal and smooth out the edges of the layout. [10b]

Remove any wool from the netting that has attached in the rubbing phase, then place the netting back on the project. Rub it down one last time with the hand-felting tool, especially in the areas that were coming up from the silk and need more attention.

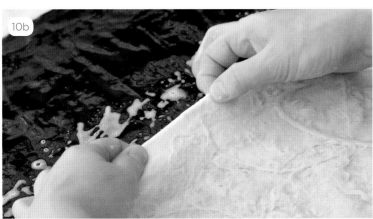

11) Remove the netting. Tuck overlying pieces of fabric, also known as the seams, underneath the plastic resist.

Flip the pattern over. [11]

12) Open the seams back up after you flip the pattern. (You flip the seams over initially when you flip the pattern, so that the layout will stick to the resist when flipping.) Lay out the front right vest panel with silk gauze material. Make sure the silk panel lines up along the edges of the pattern seam and does not have any overhang. Line up the bottom-edge length and the top of the collar with the back side of the layout (use the seams as a guide).

When cutting the silk panel edge, line up the silk so it is vertically straight and is 16½ in. wide. This width will allow enough material for the panels to overlap when finished. [12a–b]

At the neckline, cut a curve in the silk panel to create curved edges in the neckline. At the bottom left side of the panel, cut another curve in the silk panel so the bottom panel edge will be curved, and not pointy, when finished. (See sketch on page 76 for panel dimensions.)

13) Begin laying wool out on top of the silk panel as in step 3. Along the seam edges, lay a 1 in. wide layer of wool, half as thick as the main panel layout. The seam will be joining this thinner layer, and you don't want the final seam to be too thick. Lay the wool out along the contours of the pattern. [13]

14) Flip over the right-side seams of the vest. [14a] At the corners where the neckline and shoulder meet, cut a small slit into the piece at a 45° angle, stopping the slit ¼ in. before the pattern edge. [14b]

Flip the shoulder, arm, and neck seams onto the other side of the pattern, over the top of the wool.

Lightly stretch the wool from the felted seam onto the front panel wool layout, to even out and blend the fibers. [14c] Lay a dust layer of roving over the top of the seam and panel layer of wool. [14d] Tuck wool under the silk material on the edges of the layout.

Dry-felt the panel and look for any weak spots to repair.

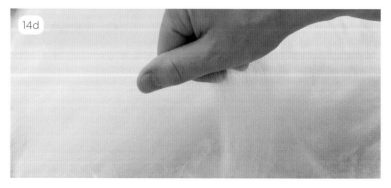

15) Lay the raw wool locks, yarn, and silk roving as in steps 5–7. Start the layout for the locks, yarn, and silk, right at the edge where they left off in the seam. [15a–b]

16) Saturate the layout as in step 8.

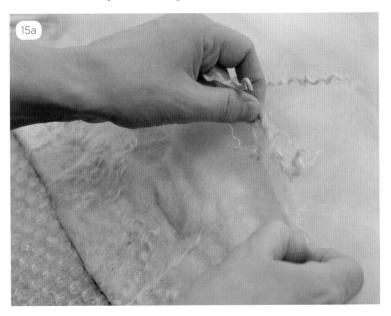

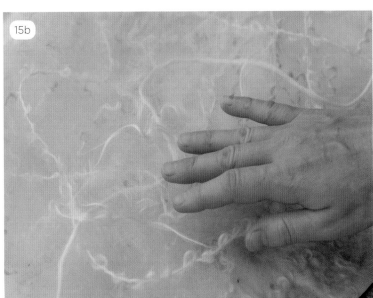

17) Cover and agitate the panel as in steps 9–10. Each time you lift the netting, crease and seal down the seams with your hand. Seal down the panel edges with your palms and fingers. [17]

18) Cover the right panel with your thinner resist layer. [18]

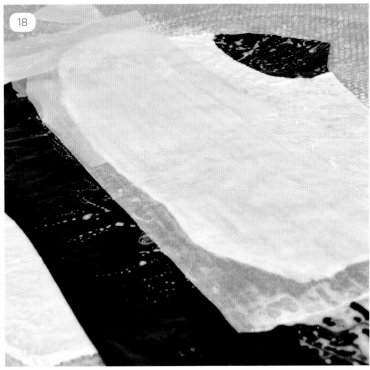

19) Lay out the silk gauze material for the left vest panel as in step 12, only mirror the layout. Measure the width and length of the right panel to make sure the left panel matches up. [19]

20) Repeat roving and fiber layout for the left panel as in steps 13–15. [20]

21) Saturate the layout as in step 8. Cover and agitate the panel as in steps 9–10. [21] After each time you lift the netting, crease and seal down the seams with your hand. Seal down the panel edges with your palms and fingers.

22) Take a plastic rolling rod and roll the bubble mat and project around the rod in the direction the project was laid out. Keep the mat tight when rolling it out. Continually straighten the fabric out as you roll it up, by lightly tugging the vest forward if it bunches. [22] Secure the roll with bubble mat ties. Tie it in a bow so it can easily be untied at the end of rolling.

Drain out any excess water by tipping the roll over the top of a bucket. Roll the mat up in a dry towel to absorb moisture.

23) Roll the project a thousand times: each roll count is from your palms to your elbows and back to your palms. This takes around fifteen to twenty minutes, depending on your speed. [23]

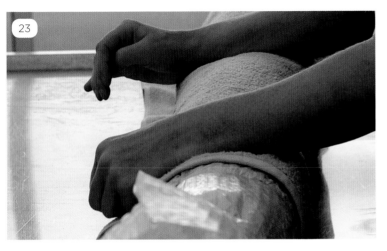

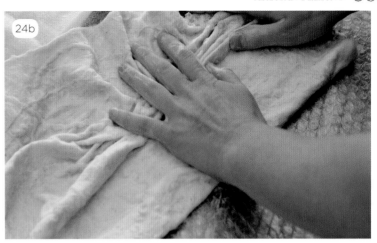

24) Unroll the mat. [24a] Begin the fulling process by rubbing your design against the plastic resist pattern and bubble mat. Rub soap on the seams and rub them well against the resist to make sure they are secure and without ridges. [24b–d]

It is important to get the project in a secure place to remove the resist without the seams coming apart. Use the palm-sized sheet of bubble wrap to further seal and smooth the seams.

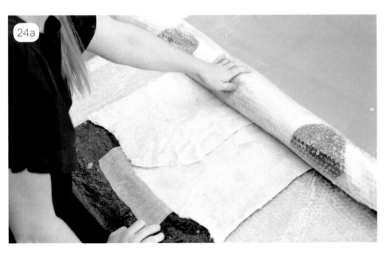

25) Gently peel the vest off the plastic resist. Continue fulling each portion of the vest, silk side down, against the bubble mat. Rub the project in vertical, horizontal, and circular motions against the bubble mat until the vest starts to feel firm and you can see the silk layer crinkle up from shrinking. [25a]

Flip the vest over and rub the wool side against the bubbles. In areas where the felt needs more fulling, roll the edges of the vest into itself twenty-five to fifty times. [25b] Rub all of the edges of the vest in a perpendicular direction on the bubble mat to firm them up and ensure there are no loose fibers. [25c]

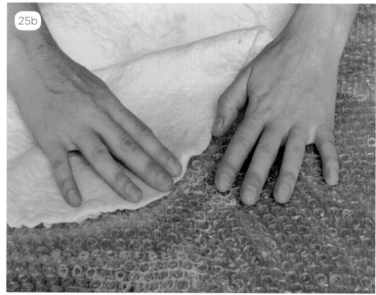

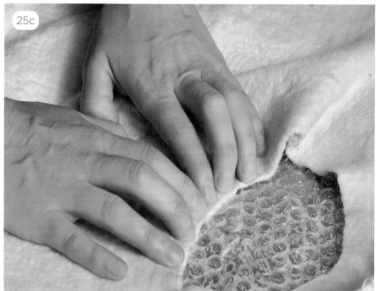

26) Ball the vest up and knead it like bread dough, one hundred times. Stretch the vest in vertical and horizontal directions to smooth out the felt texture. [26]

Knead a hundred more times. Stretch again.

27) Continue rubbing the vest in vertical and horizontal directions on the bubble mat until you feel it firm up. To get a firm neckline that stands on its own while the vest is being worn, spend more time fulling the neckline until it feels very firm.

Compare both vest panel sides to make sure they are the same in length and width. Full the vest in the direction that needs more shrinking or evening out.

Feel and look over all surfaces of the vest for any loose fibers or detached pieces of silk. Continue rubbing any areas needing more fulling until they are firm and completely fulled. The project should feel firm and not squishy before you are ready to wash out the soap.

28) With your fingertips, lightly pull up any wool locks that have become felted and embedded into the layout. This will bring out the texture of the wool locks. But pull only a part of the lock up—it must stay adhered to the vest. Do this to most of the wool locks—but not all of them—in the areas you feel need more texture. [28]

29) Create a flattering fit by bringing in the waistline of the vest. Roll the vest sides around the waistline up, and roll back and forth for fifty rolls, or until you notice shrinkage. [29] Do this also to the armpits, neckline, and any other area where you want a shapelier fit.

30) Rinse the soap from the vest with room-temperature water, then spin the water out with a spin dryer.

31) Place the damp vest onto a mannequin. The vest will have shrunk significantly at this stage, and you can stretch it out several more inches in all directions. Rub the vest against the mannequin's neck, bust, shoulders, waist, and hips to create a good fit to the body curves. [31a]

If any portions of the vest need to come in more, you can take the garment off the mannequin and rework the area on the soapy surface of the mat (remember to rinse the soap out before you place the garment back on the mannequin).

Use pins to secure the front panels together, the way you want the vest to fit when on the body. With the vest still pinned, use steam to shape the arms, neckline, bust, and waist. [31b]

32) After measuring various sections for consistency, trim any areas you think need to be adjusted in shape, width, or length. While the vest is on the mannequin, mark with pencil where you want to cut. Then, to make the cut, take the vest off the mannequin. [32]

After you cut the edge, be sure to seal the fibers up by rubbing the cut edge in a perpendicular direction against a wet and soapy area on your bubble mat. Rinse that section out again with water.

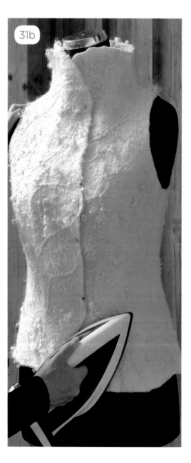

33) Use a crochet hook and the point of a needle to pull up additional wool fiber locks to increase the fur texture. But pull the fiber up no more than ¼ in. [33a–b]

34) Do final measurements while the vest is on the mannequin, and do any final stretching or shaping necessary. Let the vest dry out completely on the mannequin. [34]

Inspired by a Japanese kimono and made using habotai silk, this luxurious, lightweight, and airy tunic is predominantly silk with geometric wool strips. The material has a loose and relaxed drape that compliments the bold neckline, wide sleeves, and the obi-inspired belt that brings in and accentuates the waistline. The tunic slides over the head and does not require any zippers or buttons and is great for fall through spring seasons. Habotai silk has a particularly gorgeous sheen and crinkles when felted with wool.

Light, Airy Tunic with Belt

What you will learn:

This project teaches a valuable fiber arts technique—dyeing. Knowing how to dye your own fibers gives you a lot of freedom in color choice. Also, not only is felting with undyed fibers more cost-effective than using dyed fibers, but these fibers will felt a lot easier and more consistently than most commercially dyed fibers. Being very particular about color and felting consistency, I hand-dye most of my creations.

- How to dye a finished nuno felt garment
- How to felt with habotai silk
- How to create sleeves
- How to create a tunic pattern and belt
- How to create a geometric pattern with wool strips on silk
- How to shape and fit a tunic to the body

Material List:

- 4 yds. of 8 mm silk habotai, 55 in. wide (a.k.a. pongee silk)
- 7 oz. of undyed 19-micron merino wool
- Basic felt tools: see pages 16–21
- 60 × 75 in. sheet of 6 mm painters' plastic for resist tunic pattern

Dyeing Materials:

- Basic dyeing materials: see page 19 (e.g., electric stove burner, dye pot, mixing container, $1/8$-teaspoon measuring spoon, heavy-duty rubber gloves, wooden spoon for stirring, and vinegar)
- Sapphire-blue acid dye
- Royal-blue acid dye
- Navy-blue acid dye

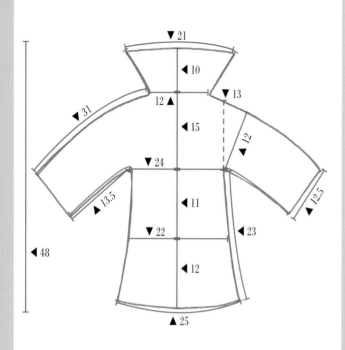

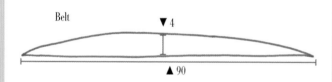

Belt

Final Width and Length
Width: 19 in. (base of tunic)
Length: 34 in. (top of collar to base)

Pattern Width and Length
Width: 25 in. (base of tunic)
Length: 48 in. (top of collar to base)

Belt Final Width and Length
Width: 2½ in. (at widest part)
Length: 80 in.

Belt Layout
Width: 4 in. (at widest part)
Length: 90 in.

Shrink Factor:
Horizontal SF (width): 1.3
Vertical SF (length): 1.4

Belt Shrink Factor:
Horizontal SF (width): 1.13
Vertical SF (length): 1.6

Horizontal Shrink Factor:
19 in. × (SF) = 25 in. → 25 in. / 19 in. = 1.3 SF
Vertical Shrink Factor:
34 in. × (SF) = 48 in. → 48 in. / 34 in. = 1.4 SF

Horizontal Shrink Factor Belt:
80 in. × (SF) = 90 in. → 90 in. / 80 in. = 1.13 SF

Vertical Shrink Factor Belt:
2½ in. × (SF) = 4 in. → 4 in. / 2½ in. = 1.6 SF

Note: The tunic's vertical SF is slightly higher because the neck was fulled longer than the rest of the tunic. Using an estimated 1.4 SF for this entire project will be sufficient.

The belt has a large vertical SF, but a small horizontal SF, since I fulled the belt more vertically and stretched the belt horizontally a lot. You can choose whether you want a thin and long belt, or thick and shorter belt, and full accordingly.

├─────┤ **Seam**
├─────────┤ **Measurements in Inches**

Inch / Centimeter conversion

21 / 53	12.5 / 32
10 / 25	13.5 / 34
12 / 30	22 / 56
31 / 79	23 / 58
13 / 33	25 / 63
15 / 38	48 / 121
13 / 33	4 / 10
24 / 61	90 / 228
11 / 28	

1) Create your tunic pattern out of 6 mm resist pattern plastic. On page 92 is a sketch of the pattern with the dimensions used in the project. (The pattern shown in the project photos shows longer sleeves and neckline than in the sketch, allowing for modifications.) The pattern for this tunic fits size small to medium, depending on how you like the fit. This project has about a 1.4 shrink factor, including the shrinking that will take place in the dye pot. Make any desired modifications to your pattern. (See pages 30–35.)

2) Using the template, begin by laying the habotai silk onto the base of your pattern. Because the pattern is so large and to reduce silk waste, I laid the silk onto the pattern in two sections. First, a large silk piece over the right arm, neck, and body. I used the excess silk from cutting out the first section to create the left arm. [2a]

At the pattern seams, allow a 1½ in. overlay of silk material over the pattern edge. For the edges, cut right in line with where you want the edge to be (e.g., the bottom edge, neckline, and armholes). [2b]

Make sure, when connecting the two pieces of silk, to allow for a 1 in. overlay at the connection point. Lay a thin strip of roving about ½ in. wide between the connecting silk pieces. Flatten and widen out the thin piece of roving; make sure it is not twisted. [2c]

Lay a 1 in. roving strip on top, allowing the roving to cover halfway onto the left arm, and halfway onto the large silk piece. This will fuse the two pieces of silk together in the later felting stages and hide any silk edges. [2d–e]

Sprinkle water on top of the wool and silk so the fabric does not shift when laying wool on top.

2a

2c

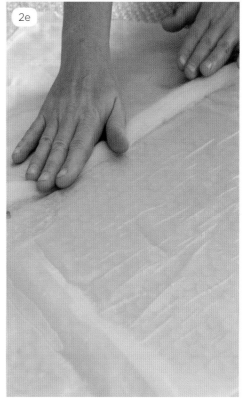
2e

2b

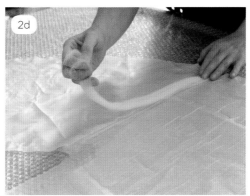
2d

3) Rip approximately fifty strips of wool roving that vary in thickness between ¾ and 1 in., and in length 10–32 in. You can get five or six strips of roving from one whole roving strand. [3a]

Place the fifty strips on a dry area of the table that will not get wet in the layout and wetting-down phases. [3b]

4) Start laying out the fifty roving strips in a triangular pattern on top of the silk base. [4a] Keep the roving flat against the silk, since the strips have a tendency to twist up when you lay them. The 8 mm habotai silk can be challenging to work with, since the weave is tighter than silk gauze. Making sure your roving is flattened out and not twisted will really help the wool bond with the silk when you start rubbing and fulling. [4b] Widen and flatten the strips by lightly spreading out the roving strands that need flattening. [4c]

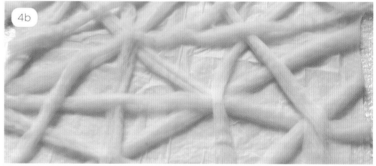
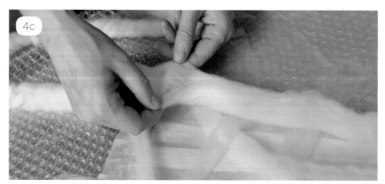

5) Lightly pull off the end of the wool strands at connecting points to make them the right length—don't cut them. At intersecting points, put a light dust layer over the top of the roving pieces, working in the direction of the bottom roving piece to fuse the crossing wool pieces together. Remember that the triangle patterns will shrink, so account for how big or small you want the triangles to be. The bigger the triangles, the more the silk will show; the smaller the triangles, the more wool you'll see. [5]

6) Create the edging along the tunic with strips of roving; however, do not lay wool layers on the seams—the seams will be created when you flip the piece. The wool edge should line up with the silk edges without any overlay. [6a]

Using scissors, snip off any pieces of wool that are extending beyond the wool-edged boarder. Make sure the snipped wool lines closely up with the silk and wool edge. [6b]

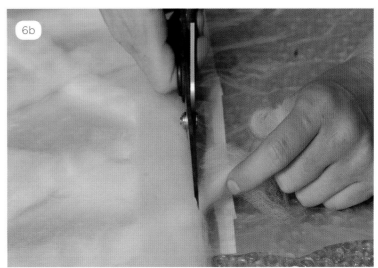

7) Lightly sprinkle water on top of the wool at a 90° angle, so the wool does not shift during saturation. You are wetting down only the wool portion of the layout, so it requires a lot less water than other layouts using mostly wool. Avoid puddles and overwatering, since too much water will shift the wool strips around and prevent the wool from bonding to the silk. [7a]

Review the design to see if you are happy with the geometric patterns, and adjust as you see fit. [7b–c]

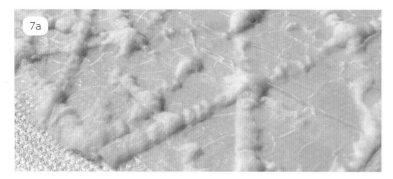

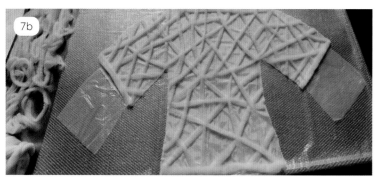

8) Cover the project with the felt netting. Rub or disperse soap over the top of the netting onto each wool strip, allowing the soap to seep through. [8a]

Use a hand-felting tool to gently agitate the strips of wool in the direction they were laid out. Start with the edges and work your way into the center of the piece. Be very gentle and careful not to push the wool edge off the silk when rubbing the edges. [8b]

9) After about ten to fifteen minutes of gentle agitation, carefully remove the felt netting. Hold one hand down on the layout while you lightly jiggle the felt netting off. Be very slow and gentle when removing the netting, since the strips come up and off easily. [9a]

Place your fingers over any areas where the wool strips are coming off the silk, and lightly rub them down. The roving strips tend to widen and spread out during the rubbing phase, so you need to nudge the wool back into a straight line. Use your fingertips to smooth out each wool strip and create a defined triangle shape. [9b]

10) Seal and smooth out the edges of the layout. Remove any wool from the netting that has attached in the rubbing phase. Place netting back on the project and rub it down one last time with the hand-felting tool, especially in the areas where the wool is coming up from the silk. It takes a lot of time and patience to work with this design to ensure that the wool bonds with the silk. [10]

11) Remove the netting. If any of the wool on the silk edges came off in the rubbing phase, place the wool strip back on the silk. Add a dust layer over the top of the wool that came off and the silk layer, and go over this portion once more with the netting and hand-felting tool. If the wool edge that came off will not adhere to the silk, you may have to cut it off and place another wool strand on the edge and refelt it.

12) Tuck the seams underneath the plastic resist. Carefully flip the pattern over by grabbing the edges at the shoulder and waistline. When it is flipped, smooth out the pattern.

13) Trim to even out the seams and to get rid of excess wool. [13a]

At the corners where the neckline and shoulder meet, and also at the centers of the armpits, cut small slits into the piece at 45° angles, stopping the slit ¼ in. before the pattern edge. [13b–c]

14) At the places where the slits were cut, add an additional layer of wool to make up for the new gap created by the cut. [14a]

Lay thin and flat strips of wool on top of the seams. These should be half as thick as the strands used in the pattern. Widen and flatten out the roving strips on top of the seams. [14b]

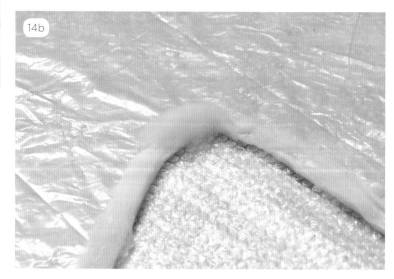

15) In the same way as in step 2, lay out the habotai silk on the other side of the tunic. [15a] However, on this side you will not allow the silk to have an overhang on the seams, but instead cut the silk exactly in line with the pattern edge. [15b–d] The layout on this side should line up with the layout you can see through the pattern.

Cover the seams with an additional roving layer on top of the silk piece. This will create a sandwich effect and seal both sides of the silk together, at the same time as creating a seamless finish.

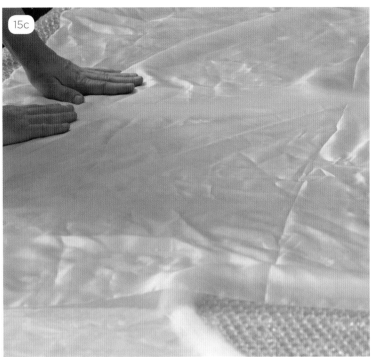

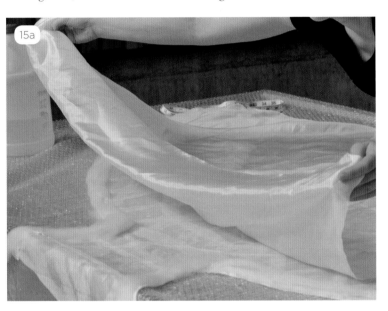

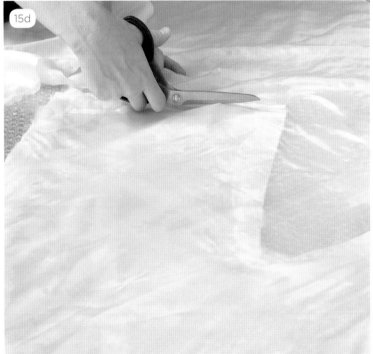

16) Rip fifty more strips of wool as in step 3. [16]

17) Lay out triangular patterns on this side as in steps 4–7. [17a–c]

18) Saturate the design with water and agitate it with the hand-felting tools, as before in steps 8–12. [18a] When rubbing the wool, focus on the seams first to make sure they are sturdy and connected. [18b] Then move on to the edges and middle parts of the design. After the final rubbing of the wool, remove the netting.

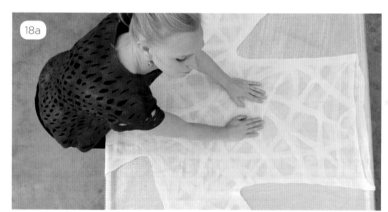

19) For the belt, lay out a long, silk length, 4 × 90 in. You can piece together several silk trimmings from your project to form this long belt. Cut curves at the ends of the silk piece. Overlap each silk piece by ½ in. and wet the silk surface down so it doesn't shift.

You will probably have to work in several sections on the table because of the length. Lay a medium weight of undyed merino wool on top of the silk base, allowing ¼ in. to come off the edges. [19a]

Wet the wool down. Seal the overhanging edges of wool underneath the silk base layer.

Cover the belt with felt netting, apply soap, and rub the surface with a hand-felting tool until it becomes solid enough to roll. [19b] Place the belt onto the felting mat next to the tunic. You will need plastic resist layers to fold the belt over so it fits inside the mat for rolling.

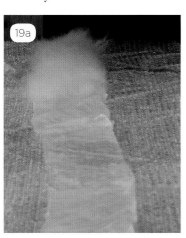

20) Take a plastic rolling rod and roll the bubble mat and project around the rod in the direction in which it was laid out. Keep the mat tight when rolling it out, and straighten the work as needed while you roll it up, by lightly tugging the tunic forward if it bunches. Secure the roll with bubble mat ties. Tie in bows so they can easily be undone at the end of rolling.

Drain out any excess water by tipping the roll over the top of a bucket. Roll the mat up in a dry towel to absorb moisture. [20]

21) Roll the project a thousand times: each roll count is from your palms to your elbows and back to your palms. This takes up to twenty minutes depending on how quickly you roll.

22) Unroll the mat. Begin the fulling process by gently rolling all of the seams. [22a] Rub soap on the seams and rub them gently against the resist and bubble mat to make sure they are secure and without ridges. [22b–c, overleaf] Use the palm-sized sheet of bubble wrap to further seal and smooth the seams. When this is done, move your hands farther onto the project and gently rub against the resist. Rub the entire surface area, on both front and back, then get it in a secure place so you can remove the resist.

If any wool strips have come off the silk, smooth them down against the silk with your fingers. Cover the wool strip with felt netting and soap and rub over them again with a hand-felting tool to get them to seal down.

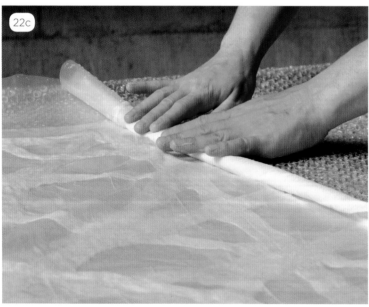

23) Gently peel the tunic off the plastic resist. As you hold the bottom of the pattern up, carefully peel the tunic off the pattern. [23a] This will turn the garment inside out and allow you to continue fulling the tunic silk side down against the bubble mat. Working with this combination of 8 mm habotai silk and wool will require a lot of patience, time, and care in the following fulling process, to ensure the wool and silk fibers bond together and the wool does not come off.

Rub both the front and back of the tunic in vertical, horizontal, and circular motions against the bubble mat until the tunic starts to feel firm and you can see the silk layer crinkle up from shrinking. [23b]

Roll up the sleeves and roll them each about fifty times. Do this both on the front and back of the tunic. In areas where the felt needs more fulling, roll the edges of the tunic inward between twenty-five and fifty times. [23c]

Flip the tunic inside out and rub the wool side against the bubbles. On the bubble mat, rub all the edges of the tunic in a perpendicular direction to firm them up and ensure there are no loose fibers.

24) Rub the belt against the bubble mat as in step 23.

25) Ball the tunic and belt up, then lightly toss them a hundred times. At this point, the tunic and belt have shrunk significantly. Stretch the tunic and belt in vertical and horizontal directions to smooth out the felt texture. Knead them a hundred more times. Stretch again. [25]

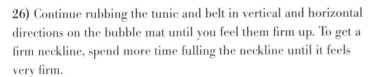

26) Continue rubbing the tunic and belt in vertical and horizontal directions on the bubble mat until you feel them firm up. To get a firm neckline, spend more time fulling the neckline until it feels very firm.

Compare both arms to make sure they match in length and width. Roll and rub the arms in the direction they need to shrink, to even the sides out. Full and stretch the tunic in the direction that needs more shrinking or evening out. [26a]

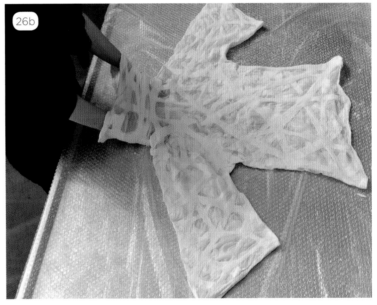

Feel and look at both sides of the tunic surfaces for any loose fibers or pieces of wool detached from the silk. Continue rubbing any areas needing more fulling until they are firm and completely fulled. The wool strips should feel firm, securely attached to the silk, and not squishy before you are ready to wash out the soap. [26b]

27) Rinse the soap from the tunic and belt with room-temperature water, and while still wet, place them into a bucket of room-temperature water. It is important that the fibers are fully saturated before being added to the dye pot for even distribution of dye color.

28) If weather permits, set your dye station up outside, or if indoors, in a well-ventilated space. Fill up a large (minimum 20 quart), stainless-steel dyeing pot, three-quarters full of water. Heat the water to about 180°F on an electric portable stove. This temperature should be too hot to touch with your bare hands, but not boiling.

I use acid dyes for all of my nuno felt projects since they will dye protein fibers (fibers from an animal), which are both wool and silk. Dyeing with acid dyes requires setting the color with hot water (or steam) and vinegar (or citric acid). The ratio of dye powder used to the weight of dry fabric is 2–4 percent of the dry weight of the fabric in dye powder. Use about 3 percent of the dry fabric weight in dye powder for this project—this equates to about 1¼ teaspoons of dye for a 7 oz. tunic. [28]

29) While wearing your mixing gloves, scoop out the desired amount of acid dye into the mixing container in ⅛-teaspoon increments. I used six scoops of royal-blue acid dye, three scoops of sapphire-blue acid dye, and one scoop of navy-blue acid dye. [29a]

Scoop out some water from your pot into the container to dissolve the dyes. Stir the dye and water in the mixing container well before pouring this mixture into the pot. [29b] Then stir the pot really well to allow the dye powder to completely dissolve. [29c] If the dye does not completely dissolve before you add the fibers, you will end up with unattractive flecks of inconsistent color, especially on the silk.

28

30) Take a test strip of felted wool and dip it into the pot to see if the color is dark enough. [30] The final dye result will be much darker than this first test dip, so envision the color two shades darker. Your colors may vary from the provided recipe, depending on the pH level of your dye water. If desired, add more dye powder directly to the pot but dissolve it well.

31) When you are happy with the dye bath color, put on your thick, heavy-duty rubber gloves. Begin with the belt and fully immerse it, then massage it in the dye bath to fully disperse the dye throughout the belt. [31a] Next, add the tunic and fully immerse and massage the piece into the dye. [31b] It is important to gently massage the felt pieces in the dye bath, since the agitation and hot water will continue to shrink the wool.

The garment will shrink by about 10 percent after the dyeing process, and it is best not to exceed this amount. When the dye is fully saturated into the garment and belt, add about a ½ cup of vinegar to the pot. [31c and d] Stir the vinegar in with your gloved hand and lightly massage the fibers again to make sure the vinegar evenly disperses onto the garment.

Watch the color of the dye on the garment—the vinegar will add several shades. Submerge the tunic into the pot and do not allow any part of it to float to the surface. [31e, see overleaf] The more air in the project, the more it will float. To get rid of the air, massage the fibers under the water some more. [31f]) Cover the pot lid and let the tunic rest in the hot pot. If the water starts to boil, turn down the heat.

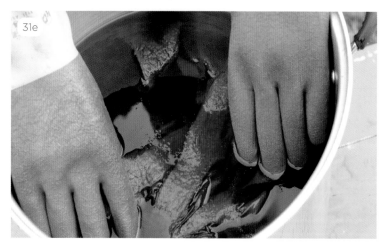

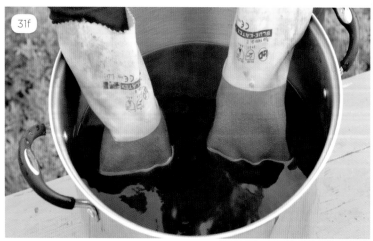

32) Every twenty minutes, massage the garment in the pot and observe the garment color. [32a] Check the water color to see how clear it is. The clearer the better, since this means that the wool and silk fibers have absorbed the dye bath. [32b] The project should stay on the 180°F burner for about an hour before you turn the stove unit off. Leave the pot on the turned-off burner and allow it to cool to room temperature. This will take several hours, depending on the outside temperature.

33) When the dye-bath water has completely cooled, the water inside the pot should be clear. (If the water is not clear, you probably used too much dye. If this is the case, soak the project in room temperature water for a few hours before rinsing.) Rinse the fabric in room temperature water until there is no observable dye discharge. Spin the water out with a spin dryer.

34) Place the damp tunic on a mannequin. [34a] The project shrinks up significantly after the fulling and dye bath. Begin gently stretching out the tunic's length and width on the front and back sides. Stretch out the arms and neckline, both in length and width. [34b–d]

Steam-shape the tunic while stretching it out. Stretch out the belt's length and width and press it with an iron to flatten it out. Let the tunic dry on the mannequin and leave the belt to dry flat. [34e]

This chic, 1950s-inspired bolero jacket is rich with embroidered detail and creates a classic couture look. When I design my fashion pieces, I like to borrow from the past for looks like this bolero—Audrey Hepburn would have rocked this and so will you! The silk organza jacket has an accentuated collar that draws attention to the face, features loose flared sleeves, and hits right at the waistline.

Embroidered Bolero Jacket

What you will learn:

Construct this sophisticated piece
without the countless hours
you'd have to spend doing the
embroidering yourself.

• How to felt embroidered silk
• How to create a bolero jacket
• How to shape and fit a bolero jacket
  to the body

Material List:

There are endless selections of fabric to choose
from for this project, including silk with
embroidered sequins, silk lace, textured silks, etc.
Lighter fabrics work best to compensate for the
extra weight of the embroidery.

• 2½ yds. of embroidered silk (organza, chiffon, or
  gauze). As with fabric for all nuno felt projects,

the silk must have an open weave. Be sure the
embroidery can safely get wet.

• 5 oz. of black 19-micron merino wool, or
coordinating color with your embroidered silk
• Basic felt tools: see pages 16–21
• 50 × 51 in. sheet of 6 mm painters' plastic for
resist bolero pattern
• 20 × 32 in. resist plastic, lighter weight (about
the weight of a garbage bag)

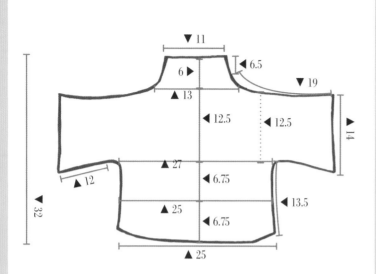

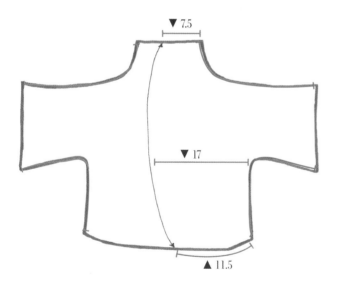

Final Width and Length
Width: 18½ in. (bolero base)
Length: 19 in. (top of collar to base)

Pattern Width and Length
Width: 25 in. (bolero base)
Length: 32 in. (top of collar to base)

Shrink Factor:
Horizontal SF (width): 1.35
Vertical SF (length): 1.68

Horizontal Shrink Factor:
18½ in. × (SF) = 25 in. → 25 in. / 18½ in. = 1.35 SF

Vertical Shrink Factor:
19 in. × (SF) = 32 in. → 32 in. / 19 in. = 1.68 SF

Note: The vertical SF is much larger than the horizontal SF because the bolero was fulled more vertically than horizontally. You can choose to full both horizontal and vertical directions of the bolero evenly if you want a similar shrink factor.

├────────┤	Seam
├────────┤	Measurements in inches

Inch / Centimeter conversion

11 / 27	13.5 / 34
6.5 / 16	6.75 / 17
6 / 15	13.5 / 34
19 / 48	25 / 63
13 / 33	32 / 81
14 / 36	7.5 / 19
12.5 / 32	17 / 43
27 / 69	11.5 / 29
12 / 30	

1) Create your bolero pattern out of 6 mm resist pattern plastic. See page 110 for a sketch of the pattern with the dimensions used in the project. (The pattern shown in the project photographs shows longer sleeves and neckline than the sketch, allowing for modifications.) Depending on your silk material, how you like the fit, and how light or heavy you lay your wool, this pattern can fit between a small and large. You may need to make modifications to your pattern (see pages 30–35).

Make a sample felt swatch with your material and desired layout thickness, to determine your shrink factor (SF) and to test whether you need to make modifications to your pattern or layout.

2) When your pattern template is created, lay the back side of your bolero first by laying the embroidered silk onto the base of your pattern, with the embroidery face down on the plastic. [2a]

On the pattern seams, allow a 1 in. overlay of silk material over the pattern edge. [2b] For the edges, cut right in line with where you want the edge to be; do this for the bottom edge, neckline, and armholes. [2c] Sprinkle water over the top of the silk fabric so it does not shift on the pattern. [2d]

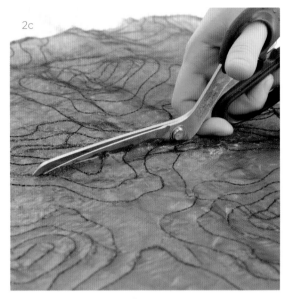

3) Lay light-medium layers of roving onto the silk along the contours of the pattern. [3a] Allow a ½ in. overhang of wool around the edges and seams of the layout. [3b] Keep the wool layers consistent. [3c]

4) When the roving is completely laid out on the back side of your pattern, begin dry-felting the wool. [4a] Look for weak spots and inconsistencies in the layout. Place dust layers over the top of the weak spots. [4b]

Tuck the wool under the base silk layer at the armhole, neckline, and bottom edges of the bolero. Make the edges smooth and straight and dry-felt over the top to secure the wool and silk. [4c]

5) Fully saturate the wool and silk fibers but avoid creating puddles in the fiber layout. [5a]

Cover the bolero with a felt netting and disperse soap and begin to rub the project with a hand-felting tool in the same direction the fibers were laid. [5b–c]

Start rubbing the edges first to make them strong and secure, then move your way toward the middle and the rest of the bolero. Vary the rubbing motions of the hand felter in circular, vertical, and horizontal motions. [5d]

6) Gently remove the felt netting after you feel the layout has come together well. Rub your hands over the wool surface, feeling for loose fibers that are not attached well enough to the silk and wool fibers. Smooth out the edges of the design with your fingers and palm. [6]

Cover the project again for one more rubdown, focusing special attention on loose fiber areas.

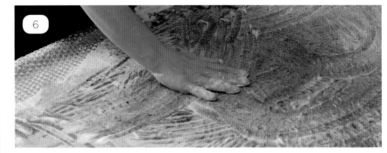

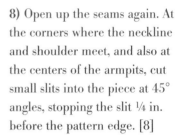

7) Fold the seams under the resist pattern. Hold the tops of the right and left shoulder, then flip the pattern and layout over. Straighten out the pattern and layout. [7]

8) Open up the seams again. At the corners where the neckline and shoulder meet, and also at the centers of the armpits, cut small slits into the piece at 45° angles, stopping the slit ¼ in. before the pattern edge. [8]

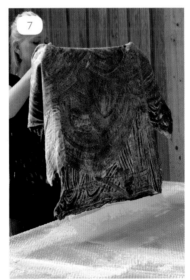

9) Lay the silk material, embroidered side facing down, on the front right panel. Line the silk up with the right-edge armhole and also with the bottom edge. [9a]

The front panel width should be 17 in. wide from the right waist edge of the pattern to the edge of the laid-out silk.

Cut curves at the bottom and at the top by the neckline. This will make the base panel measurement about 11½ in. wide and the collar 7½ in. wide from the right pattern edge. Cut the silk out along the edge of the pattern. Do not allow any silk overhang. [9b]

10) Lay a dust layer of roving along the seam edges, about the width of the seam. [10a] (The seam will be flipped over this section, and you want a dust layer of wool to connect the silk and wool together. A dust layer is sufficient to bond the fabric layers and will prevent the seams from becoming too thick.)

Flip the seams over onto the dust layer. [10b] Gently pull the overhanging wool strands out and smooth across the silk. [10c] This will thin out the wool and keep the layout consistent. At the corners of the armpit and neckline where you cut the silts, lay an additional layer of wool on top, the same amount as on the seam. Trim the bottom right corner at the base so it is straight. [10d]

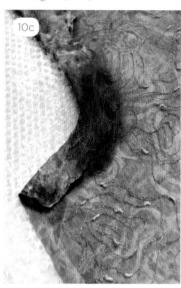

11) Lay a dust layer connecting the seam and silk layer. [11a] Begin to blanket the front panel with roving, starting at the wool edge by the seam. Lay the wool layers as you did in step 3. [11b–c]

12) Dry-felt the finished roving layout as in step 4. [12a–b]

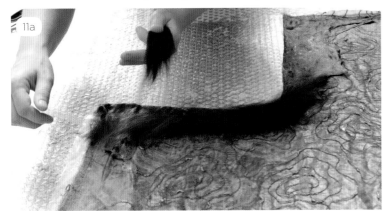

13) Saturate [13a], soap [13b], and rub the layout as in step 5. Start rubbing the seams and edges first, then move your way across the rest of the pattern.

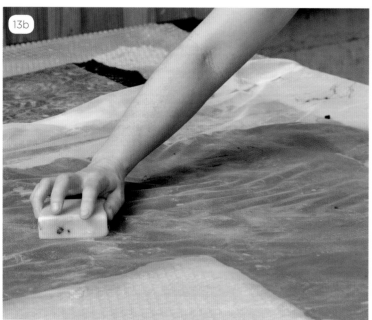

14) Remove the netting and address problem areas as in step 6. Seal the edges and seams down with your palm, including any loose fibers that are hanging off the seams. [14]

15) Cover the right panel with thin plastic resist material. Smooth out any bubbles in the plastic resist. [15]

16) Begin laying out the front left-side panel of the bolero, as in steps 9–14. [16a] Mirror the layout of the right panel. Measure out the width of the right panel to make sure the left panel matches it up. [16b–d]

17) Take a plastic rolling rod and roll the bubble mat and project around the rod in the direction the project was laid out. Keep the mat tight when rolling it out. Straighten out the fabric as necessary while you roll it up, by lightly tugging the bolero forward if it bunches. Secure the roll with bubble mat ties. [17a–b]

Drain out any excess water by tipping the roll over the top of a bucket. Roll the mat up in a dry towel to absorb moisture.

18) Roll the project a thousand times: each roll count is from your palms to your elbows and back to your palms. This takes approximately fifteen to twenty minutes, depending on how long it takes you to roll.

19) Unroll the mat. Begin the fulling process by rubbing your design against the plastic resist pattern and bubble mat. Rub soap on the seams and rub them well against the resist to make sure they are secure and without ridges. [19]

Get the project to a secure place to remove the resist so the seams won't come apart. Use a hand-sized sheet of bubble wrap to further seal and smooth the seams.

20) Gently peel the bolero off the plastic resist. Continue fulling each portion of the bolero, wool side down, against the bubble mat. Rub the project in vertical, horizontal, and circular motions against the bubble mat until the bolero starts to feel firm and you can see the silk layer crinkle up from shrinking. [20a]

Flip the bolero over and rub the silk side against the bubbles. In areas where the felt needs more fulling, roll the edges of the bolero into itself twenty-five to fifty times. [20b] Rub all the edges of the bolero in a perpendicular direction on the bubble mat, to firm them up and ensure there are no loose fibers.

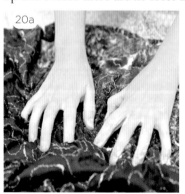

21) Ball the bolero up and knead it like bread, one hundred times. Stretch the fabric in vertical and horizontal directions to smooth out the felt texture. Knead a hundred more times if required. Stretch again. [21]

22) Continue rubbing the bolero in vertical and horizontal directions on the bubble mat until you feel it firm up. To get a firm neckline that stands on its own while the bolero is being worn, spend more time fulling the neckline until it feels extra firm.

Compare both bolero arms and panel sides to make sure they are even in length and width.

Full the bolero in any direction that needs more shrinking or evening out. Feel and look at all surfaces for any loose fibers or detached pieces of silk. Continue rubbing any areas needing more fulling, until they are firm and completely fulled. The project should feel firm and not squishy before you are ready to wash out the soap.

23) Create a flattering fit by bringing in the waistline of the bolero. Roll the sides around the waistline up, and roll back and forth for fifty rolls or until you notice shrinkage. Do this also to the armpits, neckline, and any other area that you want a shapelier fit. [23]

24) Rinse the soap from the bolero with room-temperature water and spin the water out with a spin dryer.

25) Place the damp garment onto a mannequin. [25a] The bolero will have shrunk significantly by this stage, and you can stretch it out several more inches in all directions. [25b] Rub the bolero against the mannequin's neck, bust, shoulders, waist, and hips to create a good fit to the body curves. [25c]

If any portions of the bolero need to come in more, you can take the garment off the mannequin and rework the area on the soapy surface of the mat. (Be sure to rinse the soap out before you place the garment back on the mannequin.)

26) After measuring various sections of the bolero for consistency [26a], do final stretching and shaping. If some pieces of silk did not adhere completely to the wool, repair the silk with some tight, small hand stitches in a matching thread color. [26b]

Use pins to secure the front panels together where you want the bolero to lie when on the body. Use steam to shape the arms, neckline, bust, and waist, with the bolero still pinned. [26c]

27) Let the bolero dry on the mannequin.

Spring and fall are perfect seasons for the weight of this tailored blazer, which can be worn in business settings, then dressed up or down for casual elegance. Wear it sassy with the collar up, or down and more conservative. The materials and construction of this blazer are very simple but make a subtle statement when worn.

Tailored Blazer or Jacket with Dyed Gradient

What you will learn: This project expands on the dye skills learned in Project 4: Light, Airy Tunic.

- How to dye a gradient pattern on a finished blazer
- How to create a tailored look on a blazer
- How to create nuno felt jacket lapels
- How to shape a blazer to the body
- How to apply gradient dyeing
- How to create a matching belt, similar to the one in Project 5.

Materials List:

- 3 yds. of undyed silk organza
- 15 oz. of undyed 19-micron merino wool
- Basic felt tools: see pages 16–21
- 60 × 55 in. sheet of 6 mm painters' plastic for blazer resist pattern
- 60 × 20 in. lighter-weight resist plastic (about the weight of a garbage bag)

Dyeing Materials:

- Basic dyeing materials (see page 19): Stove burner, dye pot, mixing container, 1/8-teaspoon measuring spoon, wooden spoon for stirring and vinegar
- Silver-gray acid dye
- Brown acid dye
- Olive acid dye

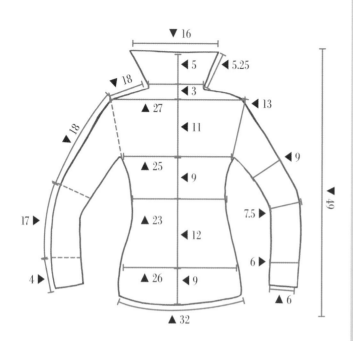

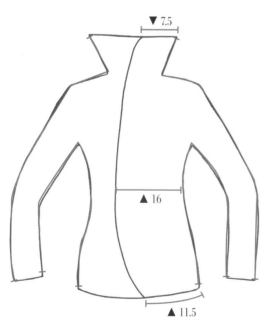

Final Width and Length
Width: 21 in. (blazer base)
Length: 32 in. (top of collar to base)

Pattern Width and Length
Width: 32 in. (blazer base)
Length: 49 in. (top of collar to base)

Shrink Factor:
Horizontal SF (width): 1.53
Vertical SF (length): 1.53

Horizontal Shrink Factor:
21 in. × (SF) = 32 in. ➜ 32 in. / 21 in. = 1.53 SF

Vertical Shrink Factor:
32 in. × (SF) = 49 in. ➜ 49 in. / 32 in. = 1.53 SF

Note: The vertical SF is the same as the horizontal SF because the blazer was evenly fulled, both horizontally and vertically.

⊢————⊣ Seam

⊢————————⊣ Measurements in inches

Inch / Centimeter conversion	
16 / 41	25 / 64
5.25 / 13	7.5 / 19
5 / 13	23 / 58
8.5 / 22	17 / 43
11 / 28	12 / 30
3 / 76	6 / 15
27 / 69	26 / 66
13 / 33	49 / 122
11 / 28	7.5 / 19
18 / 46	11.5 / 29
9 / 23	

1) Create your blazer pattern out of 6 mm resist pattern plastic. See page 122 for a sketch of the pattern with the dimensions used in the project.

This project has about a 1.53 shrink factor and the final blazer is around a size small–medium. Make any desired modifications to your pattern (see pages 30–35).

The project has a medium-light weight. You can lay heavier wool layers if you want a thicker jacket or coat feel. A heavier layout will decrease your shrink factor.

2) When your pattern template is created, begin by laying the silk organza onto the base of your pattern. Because this is such a large and wide pattern, I laid the pattern out in sections, starting with the back side of the blazer. [2a]

On the pattern seams, allow 1½ in. overlay of silk material over the pattern edge. For the edges, cut right in line with where you want the edge to be; do this for the bottom edge, neckline, and armholes.

Sprinkle water over top of the silk fabric so it does not shift on the pattern. [2b] You can piece several small pieces of silk organza together on the layout base, since the wool overlay will felt all of the adjoining pieces together—but make sure to overlap each adjoining silk piece by ¾ in.

3) Begin by laying out the wool and rubbing down the right arm and body, before moving to the left arm section. Keeping the wool layers consistent, lay light-medium layers of roving onto the silk along the contours of the pattern. Allow a ½ in. overhang of wool around the edges and seams of the layout. [3]

4) When the roving is completely laid out, begin dry-felting the wool. Look for weak spots and inconsistencies in the layout. Place dust layers over any weak or thin areas. [4]

Tuck the wool under the base silk layer at the armhole, neckline, and bottom edges of the blazer. Make the edges smooth and straight and dry-felt over the top to secure the wool and silk.

5) Fully saturate the wool and silk fibers but avoid creating puddles in the fiber layout.

Tuck the edges of wool under the silk base. [5a] Cover the blazer with a felt netting and disperse the soap. [5b–c]

Begin to rub the project with a hand-felting tool in the same direction the fibers were laid. Start rubbing the edges first to make them strong and secure, then move your way throughout and toward the middle. Vary the rubbing motions of the hand felter in circular, vertical, and horizontal motions. [5d]

6) Gently remove the felt netting after you feel the layout has come together well. Rub your hands over the wool surface feeling for loose fibers that are poorly attached to the silk and wool fibers. [6a]

Smooth out the edges of the design with your fingers and palm. Cover the project again for one more rubdown, focusing special attention on any loose-fiber areas. [6b]

7) Fold the right arm over the layout body. [7a] Shift the pattern on the table to make room for the left arm. Place silk organza over the top of the left arm as before in step 2. [7b]

Begin laying the wool out as in step 3. Start laying the wool at the edge where you left off in the first section. Repeat steps 4–6 on the left arm. [7c]

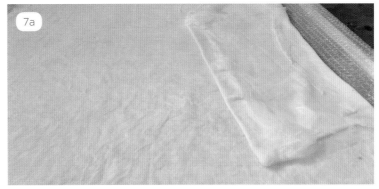

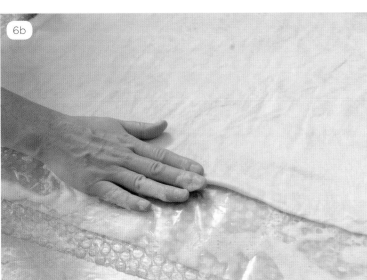

8) Fold the seams under the resist pattern, then smooth them out with your hands. [8a]

Hold the tops of the right and left shoulder and flip the pattern and layout over. Straighten out the pattern and layout once flipped. [8b]

9) Open up the seams again. [9a] At the corners, where the neckline and shoulder meet, and also at the centers of the armpits, cut small slits into the piece at 45° angles, stopping the slit ¼ in. before the pattern edge. [9b]

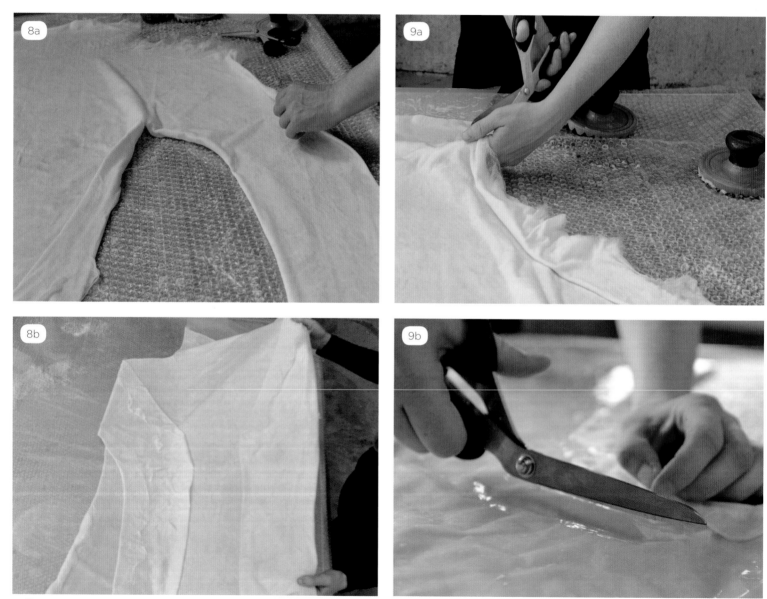

10) Lay out the silk organza for the left blazer panel. Line the silk's edge with the left edge of the pattern, and in line with the top collar edge and the bottom edge of the pattern. [10a]

Lay silk on the left arm along the pattern edges. Do not allow any silk overhang. The front panel width should be 16 in. wide from the left waist edge of the pattern to the edge of the laid-out silk.

Cut curves at the bottom and at the top by the neckline. This will make the panel measurement about 11½ in. wide at the bottom, and 7½ in. wide at the neckline from the left pattern edge. [10b]

11) Lay a dust layer of roving about the width of the seam, along the seam edges. [11a] This is sufficient to bond the silk fabric layers and will prevent the seams from becoming too thick. Flip the seams over onto the dust layer. [11b]

Gently stretch the overhanging wool strands out and smooth across the silk base layer. This will thin out the wool and keep the layout consistent. [11c]

At the corners of the armpit and neckline where you cut the slits, lay an additional layer of wool on top, the same amount as on the seam. Trim the bottom left corner at the base so it is straight.

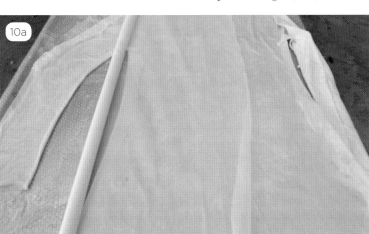

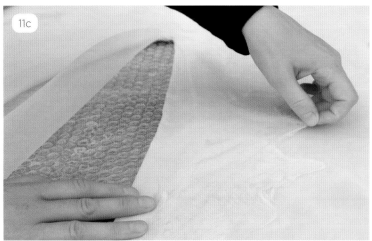

12) Lay a dust layer connecting the seam and silk layer. Begin to blanket the front panel with roving, starting at the wool edge by the seam. Lay the wool layers as before in step 3. [12]

13) Dry-felt the finished roving layout as in step 4.

14) Saturate, soap, and rub the layout as in step 5. [14a–b] Rub the seams and edges first, then the rest of the pattern.

15) Remove the netting and address problem areas as in step 6. Seal down the edges and seams with your palm, including any loose fibers that are hanging off the seams.

16) Cover the left panel with thin plastic resist material. Smooth out any bubbles in the plastic resist. [16]

17) Begin laying out the front right-side panel of the blazer as in steps 10–15. Mirror the layout of the left panel. Measure out the width of the right panel to make sure the left panel measurements match up. [17a–d]

18) Take a plastic rolling rod and roll the bubble mat and fabric around the rod in the direction the project was laid out. [18] Keep the mat tight when rolling. Straighten out the fabric as needed as you roll it up, by lightly tugging the blazer forward if it bunches. Secure the roll with bubble mat ties.

Drain out any excess water by tipping the roll over the top of a bucket. Roll the mat up in a dry towel to absorb moisture.

19) Roll the project a thousand times: each roll count is from your palms to your elbows and back to your palms. This takes approximately fifteen to twenty minutes, depending on how long it takes you to roll. [19]

20) Unroll the mat. Begin the fulling process by rubbing your design against the plastic resist pattern and bubble mat. Rub soap over the seams and rub them well against the resist to make sure they are secure and without ridges. [20a]

Get the project to a suitable place to remove the resist so the seams will not come apart. Use a palm-sized sheet of bubble wrap to further seal and smooth the seams. When you see significant crinkling in the silk organza, it is safe to remove the resist. [20b]

21) Gently peel the blazer off the plastic resist. Continue fulling each portion of the blazer, wool side down against the bubble mat. [21a] Rub the project in vertical, horizontal, and circular motions against the bubble mat until the blazer starts to feel firm and you continue seeing the silk layer crinkle up from shrinking.

Flip the blazer over and rub the silk side against the bubbles. Roll each sleeve up into itself twenty-five to fifty times. Repeat this rolling motion on the front and the back side of the blazer. [21b–c]

Rub all the edges in a perpendicular direction on the bubble mat to firm them up and ensure there are no loose fibers. [21d]

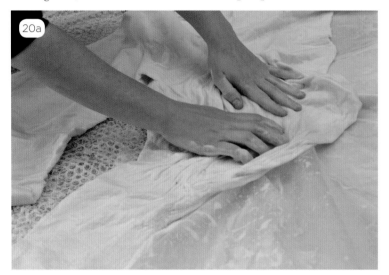

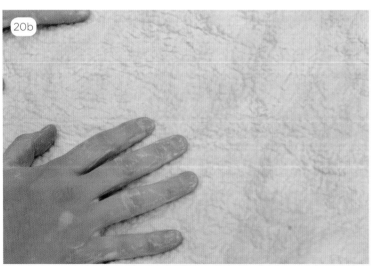

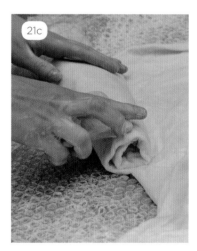

22) Ball the blazer up, then toss and knead it like bread, a hundred times. Stretch the blazer in vertical and horizontal directions to smooth out the felt texture. Knead a further hundred times if needed. Stretch again. [22]

23) Continue rubbing the blazer in vertical and horizontal directions on the bubble mat until you feel it firm up. [23] To get a firm neckline that stands on its own while the blazer is being worn, spend more time fulling the neckline until it feels extra firm.

Compare both blazer arms and panel sides to make sure they are even in length and width. Roll and full the blazer in the direction and areas that need more shrinking or evening out.

Feel and look at all surfaces of the blazer for any loose fibers or detached pieces of silk.

24) Create a flattering fit by bringing in the waistline of the blazer. Roll the sides around the waistline up, and roll back and forth for fifty rolls or until you notice shrinkage. Do this also to the armpits, neckline, and any other area that you want a shapelier fit.

To even out the sides of the blazer, stretch any needed areas a little further. This blazer requires a lot of time in the fulling stage to get the right shrinking and fit to the body. Be patient and take breaks if necessary. [24]

25) The project should feel firm and not squishy before you are ready to wash out the soap. Rinse the soap from the blazer with room-temperature water and spin the water out with a spin dryer.

26) Place the damp blazer onto a mannequin. The blazer will have shrunk significantly by this stage, and you can stretch it out several more inches in all directions. Rub the blazer against the mannequin's neck, bust, shoulders, waist, and hips to create a really good fit to the body curves.

You will probably have to continue bringing in more sections of the blazer for a good tailored fit. Take the garment off the mannequin and rework specific areas needing to be brought in. Do this on the soapy surface of the mat, by rolling and rubbing. Be sure to rinse the soap out before you place the garment back on the mannequin.

27) Use steam and your hands to shape the arms, neckline, bust, and waist. Keep checking the fit.

28) On the mannequin, open up the blazer lapels and shape them with your hands and steam them into the shape you like. Using a measuring tape and pencil, mark the areas where you want to cut the lapel. [28a] I cut the top collar lapels 5.5 in. long at 45° angles—long and very pointy. The bottom lapel cuts are 4 in. long, straight, horizontal lines. [28b] To make the sides even, after cutting out one lapel, use the triangular cutout shape as a guide for cutting out the other lapel. [28c]

Take the blazer off the mannequin and soften the pointy edges with curved cuts. [28d] Seal the cut lapel edges by rubbing them perpendicularly against a soapy, wet surface on the bubble mat. [28e]

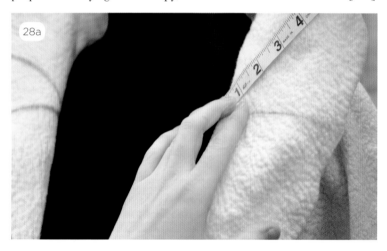

29) Do a final rinse. Place the wet blazer into a bucket for the next stage, dyeing. It is important that the fibers are fully saturated before being added to the dye pot, for even distribution of dye color. [29]

30) Set up your dye station outside, if weather permits, or indoors in a well-ventilated space. (Refer to "Light, Airy Tunic with Belt" project, step 28). Fill up a large (minimum 20 quart), stainless-steel dyeing pot, three-quarters full of water. Heat up to about 180°F.

31) Wearing your mixing gloves, scoop out the desired amount of acid dye into the mixing container in ⅛-teaspoon increments. I used only a light wash of color on this blazer, so only a small amount of pigment. The blazer color, camel, has warm and cool tones, which makes the color neutral and versatile to wear. [31]

I used two scoops of silver-gray acid dye, one scoop of brown acid dye, and ¹⁄₁₆ of a teaspoon of olive acid dye. Scoop out some water from your pot into a mixing container to dissolve the dyes. Stir them thoroughly before pouring the mixture into the pot. Slowly stir the dye into the pot to allow the dye powder to completely dissolve. If the dye does not completely dissolve before you add the fibers, you will end up with flecks of inconsistent color.

32) Take a test strip of felted wool and dip it into the pot to see if the color is dark enough. The final dye result will be much darker than the first test strip dip, so envision the color two shades darker when test dipping. Your colors may vary from the provided recipe according to the pH level of your dye water. If desired, add more dye powder directly to the pot and dissolve. [32]

33) When you are happy with the dye bath color, create a gradient dye pattern by holding the top end of the blazer and dipping the other end slowly into the dye pot. Place 5 in. of the blazer at a time into the pot. [33a]

Massage the blazer into the dye bath with one hand while holding the rest of the blazer clear of the pot with the other. [33b] Add half a cup of vinegar to the dye bath [33c] and massage the blazer well into the solution.

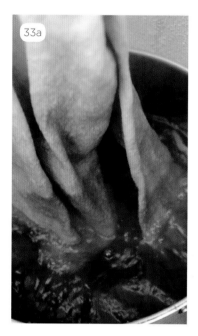

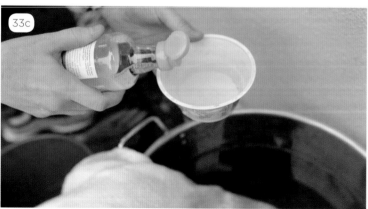

34) Every fifteen minutes, submerge 5 in. more of the blazer into the pot for a few seconds, lightly massage to allow the color to absorb [34], then pull 2 in. of the blazer out of the bath and massage the remaining 3 in. of the blazer in the dye bath. Dipping the additional 2 in. of the blazer and pulling it out will prevent stark lines from forming, and allow a gradual gradient.

Continue this dipping routine until you reach the top of the blazer. As you dip each section, the dye bath will get lighter as the colors get absorbed into the fibers. I stopped dipping the blazer at the edge of the collar to keep it white. However, by the time I got to the collar, the dye bath didn't have much color left, so it allowed a gradual color gradient at the top.

35) Turn off the burner when the entire blazer has been dyed. Allow the blazer to rest in the dye pot until it cools to room temperature.

Remove the blazer when it is cooled; rinse, spin dry, and then place it on a mannequin for final shaping. [35]

36) This project shrinks up by about 10 percent after the dye bath. Restore some of the shrunken inches by gently stretching out the blazer's length and width on the front and back sides. [36a] Stretch out the arms and neckline, both in length and width. Steam-shape the blazer while stretching it.

While it is still damp, put the blazer on your body (or someone else's body) to further stretch and shape and see how you like the fit. You may need to wet certain sections of the blazer down and full them in again for a more precise fit. [36b]

37) Measure various sections of the blazer for consistency and do any final stretching and shaping. Let the blazer dry on the mannequin. [37]

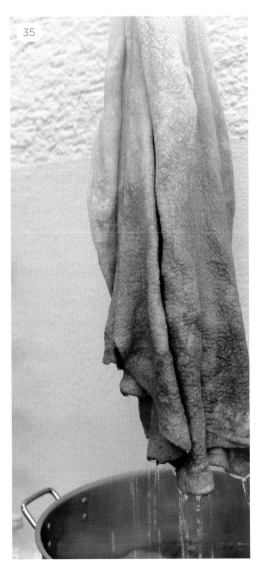

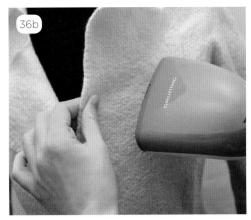
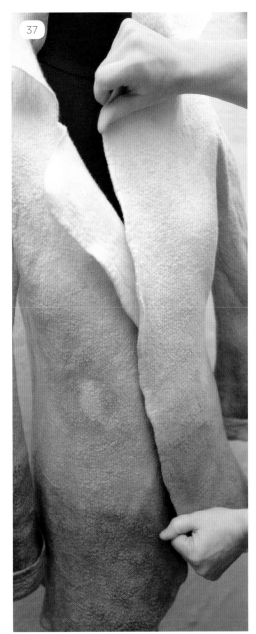

This romantic,
whimsical felt gown is
a real showstopper! It is
infinitely customizable in
length, and with sleeve
width, sequined fabric
selection, and the color
of wool roving. The
combination of sequined
fabric with silk ruching,
and gradient dyeing,
creates a truly gorgeous
gown for any formal
occasion.

Luxurious Felt Gown with Sequins and Ruching

What you will learn:

This is similar to the Tunic and Blazer projects; you get to create your own color for your garment, dyeing the silk first and then felting it to the wool. Further, these unique felt techniques can be applied to various felt projects from jackets to blouses and much more.

- How to create a gradient dye pattern with silk
- How to create a ruched texture with silk and wool
- How to felt sequined fabric onto a dress bodice
- How to create a dress pattern
- How to shape and fit a dress to the body

Material List:

- 4 yds. of 8 mm silk habotai (a.k.a. pongee silk), 55 in. wide
- ¼ yd. of silk sequined fabric
- 10 oz. of undyed 19-micron merino wool
- Basic felt tools: see pages 16–21
- 70 × 50 in. sheet of 6 mm painters' plastic for resist dress pattern (the layout is only 51 in. long, but allow extra length for future projects)
- Needle and thread to match project color
- Matching dress zipper (optional)

Dyeing Materials:

- Basic dyeing materials (see page 19): Stove burner, dye pot, mixing container, ⅛-teaspoon measuring spoon, wooden spoon for stirring and vinegar
- Sun-yellow acid dye
- Brown acid dye
- Silver-gray acid dye

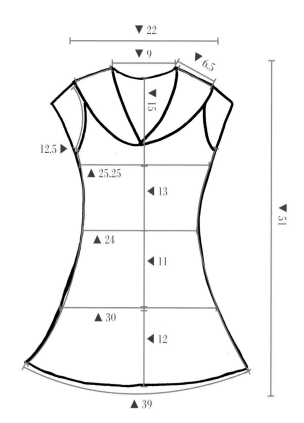

▼ 22
▼ 9
▼ 6.5
◀ 15
12.5 ▶
▲ 25.25
◀ 13
▲ 24
◀ 11
▼ 51
▲ 30
◀ 12
▲ 39

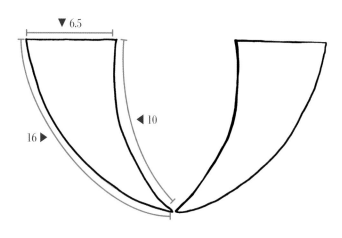

▼ 6.5
◀ 10
16 ▶

Final Width and Length
Width: 32 in. (dress base)
Length: 40½ in. (top of neck to base)

Pattern Width and Length
Width: 39 in. (dress base)
Length: 51 in. (top of neck to base)

Shrink Factor:
Horizontal SF (width): 1.22
Vertical SF (length): 1.26

Horizontal Shrink Factor:
32 in. × (SF) = 39 in. → 39 in. / 32 in. = 1.22 SF

Vertical Shrink Factor:
40½ in. × (SF) = 51 in. → 51 in. / 40½ in. = 1.26 SF
Note: The vertical SF is slightly larger than the horizontal SF because of the vertical layout of the silk material. Use 1.26 as a SF for the entire dress.

├─────────┤   Seam
├─────────┤   Measurements in inches

Inch / Centimeter conversion

22 / 56	13 / 33
9 / 23	24 / 61
6.5 / 16	11 / 28
12.5 / 32	30 / 76
16 / 41	12 / 30
10 / 25	39 / 99
15 / 38	51 / 129
25.25 / 64	

1) Begin by dying the 4 yds. of habotai silk. Assemble your dye station. Fill up a large (minimum 20 quart), stainless-steel dyeing pot, three-quarters full of water. Heat water up to about 180°F on an electric portable stove. Wash the silk with a little dish soap in the sink. Rinse out soap. Set damp silk aside.

2) The color used in this project has $1/8$ teaspoon of sun-yellow acid dye, $1/16$ teaspoon of brown acid dye, and $1/16$ teaspoon of silver-gray acid dye. Place your dye into a mixing container of hot water from the pot. [2a] Mix the water and dye well, and pour into the hot pot of water. Stir the pot well, allowing the dye to dissolve completely.

Do a test dye strip with a small piece of silk to see if you are happy with the color or need to add more pigment. Keep in mind, the final color will be two shades darker than the test swatch. [2b]

3) Next, create a gradient dye pattern by holding the top end of the silk and dipping the other end slowly into the dye pot. Place 12 in. at a time into the pot. Massage the silk with one hand, while keeping the rest of the silk clear of the pot with the other hand. Add ¼ cup of vinegar to the dye bath. Mix the dye bath well and massage the silk thoroughly. [3a–b]

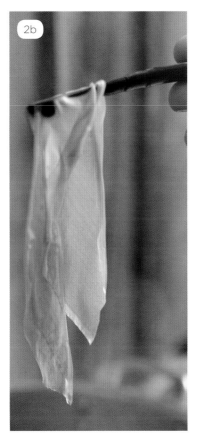

4) Every fifteen minutes, submerge 12 in. more of silk into the pot for a few seconds, then pull 5 in. of the silk out of the bath and massage the 7 in. of silk remaining in the pot in the dye bath. (Dipping the additional 5 in. of silk and pulling it out will prevent stark lines from forming and allow a gradual gradient.) Continue this dipping routine until you reach the top of the silk. [4] As you dip each section of silk, the dye bath will get lighter as the colors get absorbed into the silk.

5) Turn off the burner when the entire silk piece has been dyed. Allow the silk to rest in the dye pot until it cools down to room temperature.

Remove the silk when it is cooled; rinse, spin dry, and then hang up to dry. [5a] When fully dry, cut a variety of strips that are between 4 and 10 in. wide by 15–30 in. long. Cut the strips with the gradient running vertically on the strips. [5b–c]

6) Make your dress pattern out of 6 mm resist pattern plastic. You may want to add extra length or sleeves. See the sketch on page 138, showing the dimensions for the pattern. The pattern for this dress fits size medium, depending on how you like the fit. This project has about a 1.26 shrink factor. Make any modifications to the pattern width/length on the basis of your body size and calculated shrink factor (see pages 30–35).

7) Begin cutting out the sequined fabric for the front of the dress in the shape you want. Page 138 shows a sketch of the sequined fabric shape I made for this dress, which is meant to cover the shoulders. You can modify the shape to your liking. Allow for a 1 in. overhang on the shoulder seams. Set sequined fabric pieces aside. [7]

8) Lay a light layer of wool roving on the front side of the dress. [8a] Pay close attention to the consistency of roving layers, making sure there are no holes in the layout. [8b] At the seams, allow a 1 in. overlay of wool roving. Lay the roving right in line with the edges in a straight line. In the project photos, the sleeve lines and the bottom length of the dress are marked off with white tape. [8c]

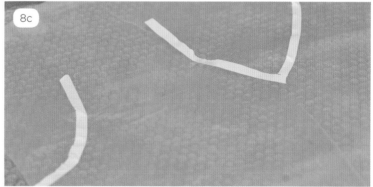

9) Dry-felt the wool and look for weak spots needing dust layers after the wool is completely laid out. [9a] Gently place the sequined fabric material (sequin side up) on top of the shoulder section, allowing for 1 in. to hang off the pattern at the shoulder seams. [9b]

Lightly dry-felt the sequined material on top of the wool roving.

10) Take the dry strips of dyed silk habotai and lightly place them strip by strip on top of the roving in a vertical pattern. [10a] Start at the bottom edge of the sequined fabric, allowing the silk strips to touch the sequined fabric but not to overlap. [10b] Create ruffles in the fabric as you place it down onto the roving by carefully scrunching the fabric up with your fingers. [10c–d]

Place lighter-gradient silk pieces next to darker gradients of color for contrast. Lay each strip barely over the top of the neighboring silk strip. Be very careful not to disturb the wool layers underneath.

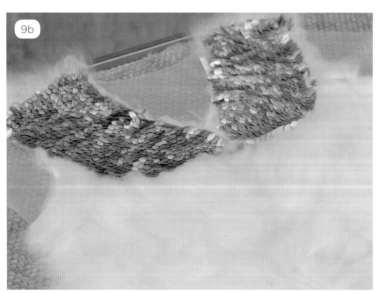

11) After all the silk ruching is covering the wool [11a], lightly dry-felt the silk pieces to the wool. Look for any gaps between each silk piece in the layout. You should see very little wool roving peaking through. Begin saturating the project with water and cover with felt netting. [11b]

12) Disperse soap on the project through the netting. [12a] Start gently rubbing the sequined fabric with a hand-felting tool through the netting. [12b] Continue rubbing down the entire dress until you feel the silk and wool coming together. [12c]

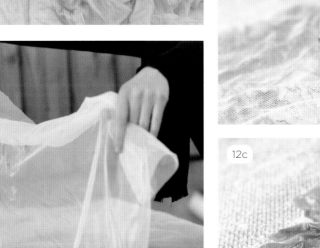

13) Remove netting. Lightly pinch and pull up the top folded layers of silk on the design, but without exposing the wool underneath. [13a] Gently rub the material against the resist to further bond the wool and silk layers. [13b]

Apply a small amount of soap onto the silk surface to encourage the fulling process. This will also allow the top layers of silk you pulled up to remain freestanding with a ruffled texture. [13c]

14) When the material feels sturdy, but not completely fulled, straighten out the dress, flip the seams over the plastic resist, and then flip the dress over to the back of the fabric. [14] To get the seams over the pattern resist, you may need to stretch the dress horizontally a little, since it will have shrunk up a bit during the fulling.

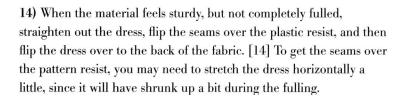

15) As in step 7, cut out your sequined fabric pattern for the back side of the dress. You may want to keep it the same shape as the front.

In this project, the back side has half the width of sequined material as the front side. The back side sequined fabric will line up with the front side sequins that are flipped over the shoulder resist. Set sequined fabric aside after cutting your desired shape.

16) Open up only the shoulder seams. Lay out the back side of the dress as in step 8. Do not lay wool off the resist; however, do place a dust layer over the top three-quarters of the seam material. [16a–c]

17) Flip the shoulder seams over and place the back side of the sequined fabric you cut on top of the wool, in line with the shoulder seam material. [17]

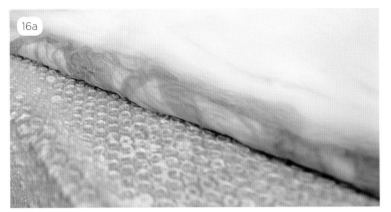

18) Dry-felt the wool layout as in step 9. Lay out the remaining silk habotai strips as in step 10. Then repeat steps 11–13.

When rubbing, start with the sequined fabric, then the seams, and then move on to the rest of the dress. When fulling the material against the resist, be very gentle to avoid disconnecting the seams. [18a–e; see overleaf]

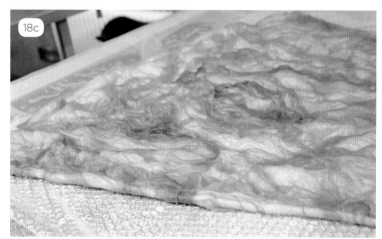

19) With a rolling rod, roll the bubble mat and project around the rod in the direction the project was laid out. Keep the mat tight when rolling it up. Straighten out the project as needed as you roll it up, by lightly tugging the dress forward if it bunches. Secure the roll with bubble mat ties. Tie the roll in bows so it can easily be untied at the end of rolling.

Drain out any excess water by tipping the roll over the top of a bucket. Roll the mat up in a dry towel to absorb moisture. [19]

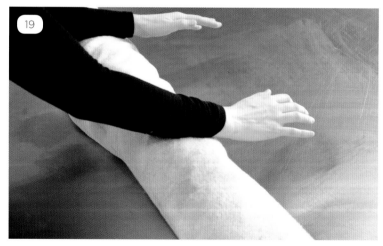

20) Roll the project a thousand times: each roll count is from your palms to your elbows and back to your palms. This takes about ten to fifteen minutes depending on how long it takes you to roll.

21) Unroll the mat. Before you begin fulling, patch up the sequined fabric with a matching thread and needle. The sequined layers may separate, and you will need to sew them back together with tight stitches. [21] If you do repair stitches at this phase, you can hide the threads when you later full this area. Also, you may see a gap in between the sequined and silk layers. If so, sew the two materials back together with neat stitches.

22) Begin the fulling process by gently rolling all of the seams. Rub soap on the seams and rub them gently against the resist and bubble mat to make sure they are secure and without ridges. [22b]

Move your hands farther onto the project and gently rub each section against the resist. Rub the entire surface area on both the front and back of the dress to get it in a secure place to remove the resist. [22c]

Roll the sides of the dress up (while still on the resist) and roll back and forth twenty-five to fifty times. [22a] If any silk strips have come off the wool, cover the area with the netting and soap and rub over them with a hand-felting tool to get them to seal down. [22d–e; see overleaf] Some pieces may have completely detached and will require repair with a needle and thread when the dress is dry.

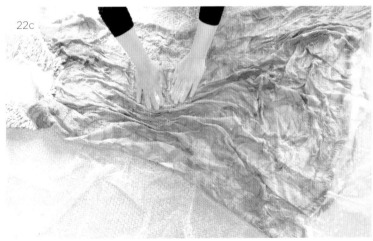

24) Ball the dress up and lightly toss it a hundred times. At this point, the dress will have shrunk significantly. Stretch the dress in vertical and horizontal directions to smooth out the felt texture. Knead it one hundred times. Stretch again. [24a–b]

23) Gently peel the dress off the plastic resist. As you hold the bottom of the project up, carefully peel the dress off the pattern. This will turn the garment inside out, so you can continue fulling the dress wool-side down against the bubble mat. [23] Rub both the front and back of the dress in vertical, horizontal, and circular motions against the bubble mat until the dress starts to feel firm and you can see the wool pucker up from shrinking.

In areas where the felt needs more fulling, roll the edges of the dress inward between twenty-five and fifty times. Flip the dress inside out.

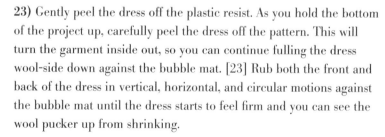

25) Roll the dress up horizontally and roll back and forth up to fifty times. Repeat in the vertical direction. Create a defined waistline by rolling the waistline edges in. [25a]

With your fingertips and nails, go over the ruffles to create more ruching. [25b]

26) When you are happy with its texture, shape, and size, rinse the soap from the dress with room-temperature water. Turn the dress inside out (to protect the sequins) and spin out excess water with a spin dryer. [26]

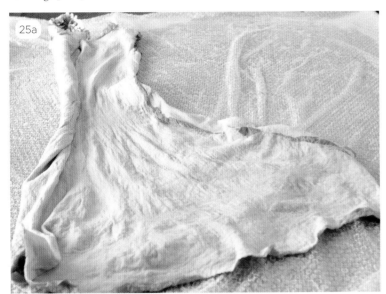

27) Place the damp dress on a mannequin. Lightly stretch the base of the dress to create more length. Steam the dress on the mannequin to give shape to all the curves at the bust, waist, hips, etc. [27a]

When dry, if there are any areas of the silk or sequined material that need repair, use a needle and matching thread to sew the piece to the wool base. [27b]

28) Optional: This dress has a wide enough opening for your head to fit through; however, if you want a more form fitted shape that will keep its profile each time you put the dress on, it would be best to sew in a side zipper on the left side. If you don't have sewing skills, you can take the dress to a trusted seamstress/tailor/friend to install the zipper for you.

PLANNING A COLLECTION

Inspiration behind the Pieces

A lot of inspiration and time goes into planning each piece even before I get to the felting table. My *Weekend in Paris Collection* took a year of off-and-on planning before I was able to even start it.

Before I start the theme of any collection, I gather a lot of inspiration from my travels. My *Weekend in Paris Collection* is a compilation of all of my weekend trips to one of my favorite cities. Since I live only a three-hour train ride away from Paris, I usually go every quarter to take in the seasonal flavors and Parisian fashion trends. I sketch my ideas in cafés, document photos from museums, take in the fragrance and rich colors of rose petals–anything and everything–to create impressions for this collection.

Throughout the year, I collect fabrics from around the United States and Europe at the various fabric stores I visit–with the collection theme in mind. Many of my silk pieces were designed and created in France and England.

When I have a good idea for a theme, I start an inspiration board that includes sketches of each garment in the collection, fabric swatches, and a color palette. I usually cut out drawings directly from my sketchbook that I

carry with me on my travels. My inspiration board has a cohesive theme and becomes a blueprint for the collection. The mood of this collection was inspired a lot by Audrey Hepburn in the 1950s in Paris. We even shot at Place du Trocadero, where Hepburn had memorable fashion shoots.

I usually draw more pieces than I end up creating. Sometimes I scrap an idea or change it into something else, as I am inspired by the creation process. I often shelf an idea that needs further development, and focus instead on the most-concrete ideas.

After the inspiration board, I create sample felt swatches I want to use throughout the collection. This is

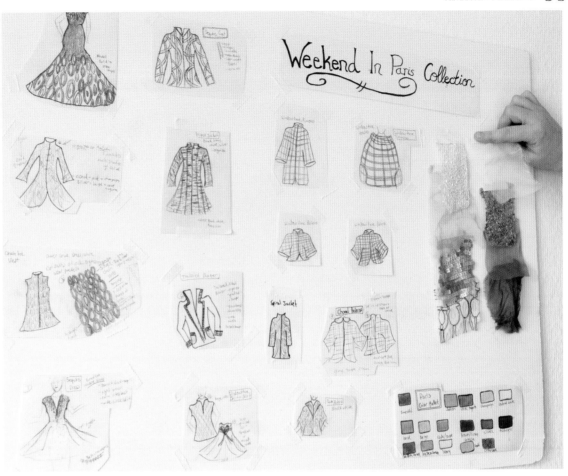

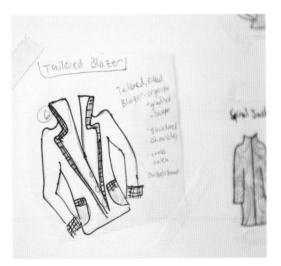

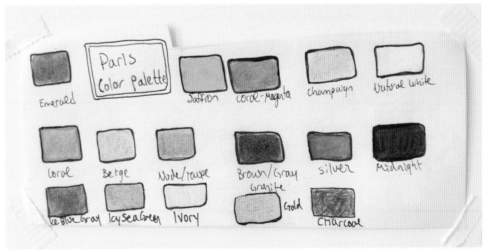

a telling process, since it gives me an accurate look into the final materials for each piece. Sometimes I think a felt technique will look amazing in combination with a felt design; I then do a sample and realize it just doesn't work, and either change the design or the fabric.

Each of these collection pieces uses the same or a similar pattern as the ones used in the seven projects in this book.

J. Hill Felt Paris Fashion Shoot Photos

Shooting a collection in the setting it was inspired by is magical! Within that context, the collection is brought to life. A photo shoot helps tell a story of the collection and all the work and inspiration that went into it. I had a team of eight artists who made this Parisian shoot happen. There was a stylist who paired 1950s-style clothing with each look, while the makeup and hair artist created looks to suit each model. The photographer chose to emphasize the theme with specific lighting and angles, at iconic places and landmarks in Paris, while the models themselves brought movement, beauty, grace, and style to each piece. The whole production team worked together to bring the collection to life—see for yourself.

◀ Window Pane Bolero Jacket, White. Made with the same pattern as the "Bolero Jacket." Materials: layout base is undyed merino wool, laid in light-to-medium-weight roving strips, on top of organza silk.

▶ Window Pane Bolero Jacket, Charcoal and Gray-Blue. Made with the same pattern as "Bolero Jacket." Materials: layout base merino wool, laid in light-to-medium-weight roving strips on top of organza silk. The charcoal bolero is dyed with silver and black acid dyes, while the gray-blue version is dyed with sapphire-blue, royal-blue, and silver acid dyes.

◀ Charcoal Brown Window Pane Kimono. Made with a modified "Bolero Jacket" pattern. This has extended and widened sleeves and is three times the length. Materials: layout base is merino wool, laid in light-to-medium-weight roving strips on top of organza silk, colored with dark-brown, black, and silver acid dyes.

▶ Tour d'Eiffel Kimono. Made with the same pattern as the "Tailored Blazer," but by extending the pattern length by 10 in. Materials: light strips of merino wool on organza. Acid-dyed coral, with red, brown, silver, pink, and yellow dyes.

◄ Midnight Blue Gown: Made with modified "Gown" dress pattern.
Materials: organza silk base, with light layers of merino wool on top.
Dyed with navy-blue, silver, and black acid dyes. Side zipper installed.

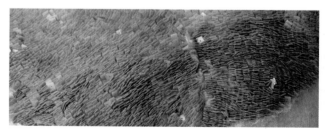

► Sequin Dress, Taupe: Made with a modified "Gown" dress pattern,
and similar felting technique. Materials: merino wool base, silk gauze
on top, and taupe sequin silk fabric on the bodice. Dyed taupe with
brown, silver, and silver-gray-green acid dyes. Side zipper installed.

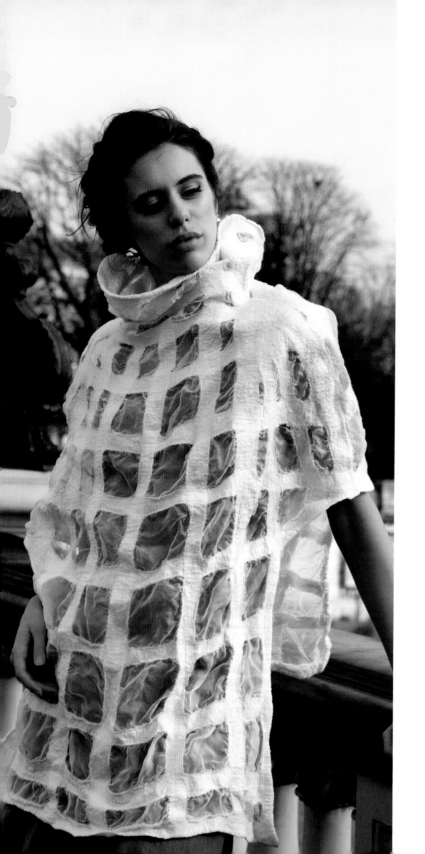

◀◀ Window Pane Poncho, White. Made with the "Poncho" pattern. Materials: undyed light-to-medium-weight strips of wool on top of silk organza.

◀ Audrey Lace Bolero: Made with same pattern and techniques as in "Bolero Jacket," with modified, lengthened sleeves. Materials: layout base is merino wool, laid in a light-to-medium-weight on the base of cotton lace fabric.

▶ Louvre Geometric Blazer. Made with same pattern as "Tailored Blazer." Materials: undyed merino wool base, silk organza top.

◀ Geometric Shawl. Materials: predyed merino wool strips on top of predyed organza silk base. Final dimensions: 32 × 75 in.

▶ La Vie en Rose Blouse, Petal Skirt & Belt. Blouse made with the same pattern as used in "Vest." Materials: lightweight merino wool on organza silk. Skirt made with modified version of the skirt portion of "Gown" pattern. Materials: medium-weight merino wool base, organza silk on top. The belt is made with organza silk and merino wool in medium-weight layout. Acid dyed with crimson, navy, silver, and brown dyes. Side zipper installed in skirt.

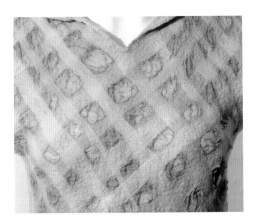

REFERENCES & ACKNOWLEDGMENTS

Nuno-Felting Resources

These are some of my favorite shops to buy nuno felt–related materials and supplies. However, be sure to check out as many local vendors as possible, including fiber arts festivals. You will soon find your own favorites and build your own resource list. Happy shopping!

Ashland Bay, Lake Oswego, Oregon
The largest wholesale fiber-and-yarn company in North America offers undyed yarns, roving, and batts.
www.ashlandbay.com

Britex Fabrics, San Francisco, California
A luxury fabric shop offering a wide selection of printed silks and sequined silk fabrics.
www.britexfabrics.com

Broadwick Silks, London, England
This fabric store is owned by the Silk Society. It also carries a variety of embroidered silk fabrics and laces.
www.broadwicksilks.com

Dahrma Trading Company
An online fiber arts retailer that sells many things, from silk, acid dye, yarn, and undyed wool to silk roving.
www.dharmatrading.com

Delectable Mountain Cloth, Brattleboro, Vermont
Gorgeous selection of specialty silk fabrics from around the world. They ship worldwide.
www.delectablemountain.com

HeartFelt Silks, Bayport, Minnesota
Owners Robbin and Harry Firth supply various felting supplies, such as their handcrafted Patented Palm Washboard® tools for felting, hand-dyed wool, silk fibers, and fabrics. They also offer felt tutorials and felting workshops at their gallery/studio.
https://heartfeltsilks.com

Mood Fabrics, New York, New York
A very exciting place to visit, especially if you watch *Project Runway*. Mood Fabric has a huge selection of silk and cotton fabrics great for nuno felting. Their online selection is great too.
www.moodfabrics.com

Paradise Fibers, Spokane, Washington
A fiber arts retail store that offers various dyed and undyed wool rovings and yarn. They offer felting supplies too. Online orders can be shipped worldwide.
www.paradisefibers.com

The Silk Society, London, England
A very high-end fabric store with a beautiful selection of embroidered silk fabrics and laces.
www.thesilksociety.com

Top Fabric of Soho, London, England
Owned by the Silk Society, it offers a large online selection of silk fabrics for those unable to visit their stores. They ship worldwide.
www.topfabric.co.uk/

WollKnoll, Oberrot-Neuhausen, Germany
They offer dyed and undyed roving, batts, yarn, and a wide selection of felting supplies, including Ashford Dye Company acid dyes, olive oil soap, felt netting (titled synthetic gauze in their catalog), hat forms, natural dyes, and so much more! It is definitely worth a trip if you are in southern Germany, especially to take a workshop and shop. They ship worldwide and have outstanding prices and selection.
www.wollknoll.eu/shop

Felters' Gatherings, Felt Centers, and Workshops:

It is important to find your felting tribe, whether online on Facebook groups or especially in person. Look for your local felting groups and gatherings. Below are international felt gatherings and centers that offer a unique way to connect with other felt makers and accomplished felting instructors.

Felter's Fling, Silver Bay, New York
A weeklong felters' gathering that offers workshops from US and international felt makers. The event offers instruction, discovery, and comradery with other felt artists around the world.
https://feltersfling.com

Felters Rendezvous, Colorado
A yearly felters' gathering featuring workshops from US and international felt makers. The weeklong event offers instruction, discovery, and comradery with other felt artists around the world.
www.thefeltingsource.com

Vrouw Wolle, Essen, Belgium
An amazing group of felt makers who offer master classes, felting events, and workshops year-round at their felting studios in northern Belgium.
*www.vrouwwolle.be/e*n

WollKnoll, Oberrot-Neuhausen, Germany
Located in picturesque rural southern Germany, they offer year-round felting workshops and events at their store and felting center. Additionally, they offer a felt school program. Well worth the visit for all felt enthusiasts!
www.wollknoll.eu/shop/info/kurse.html

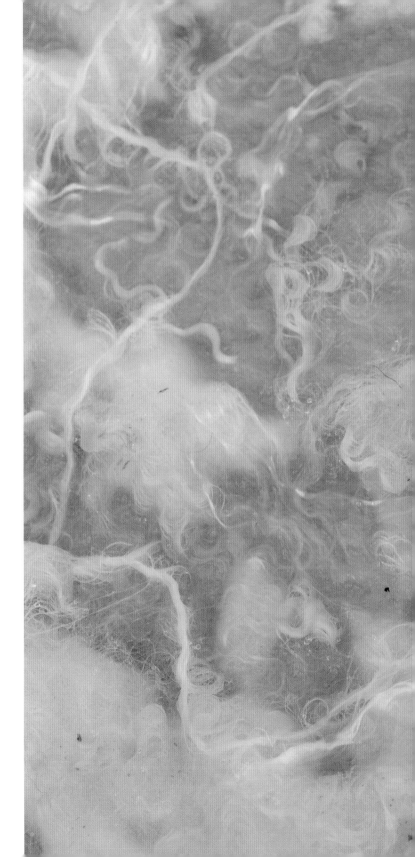

About the WollKnoll

The WollKnoll is located in picturesque rural Oberrot-Neuhausen, Germany, only one and a half hours from my home. I consider this my happy place and am very fortunate to live so close to this felters' paradise. I go there often to get the majority of my felting supplies, to felt in their workspaces as a satellite studio, and to take/give felting courses. Most of the photos for this book were taken at this inspiring location.

In 1993, owners Sonja and Bernd Fritz started the WollKnoll as a way to process their own and other farmers' raw sheep wool. The family business has grown to twenty-three employees and evolved into a felting center offering a wide range of fiber arts supplies for felters and other textile arts. They also have a felting school and year-round felting courses for all ages and experience levels. Students from around the world come here to learn felting and other related fiber arts from many internationally acclaimed felt instructors.

The WollKnoll creates many of their own, locally sourced wool blends and products according to the Standard 100 by OEKO-TEX®, an environmental-regulation standard that certifies textile companies on their ability to keep supply chains local, and textile production free of harmful chemicals.

Sonja, Bernd, and their team have generously welcomed me to the WollKnoll to do the photography for this book. I love everything they do at this center and the contribution they make to the felting community.

Jenny Hill is the founder and creative director of J. Hill Felt. Among her honors/acknowledgments are many first-place and best-in-show awards at prestigious art and design shows, including the Sausalito Art Festival, Kimball Park City Art Festival, and the Western Design Conference in Jackson, Wyoming.

She has been published in multiple industry publications, such as the *FilzFun Magazine* and the *Worldwide Colours of Felt*, and has been featured in fashion blogs, magazines, and newspapers, as well as in TV news and radio stations from Fox Network to NPR. She has been in many international fashion and art exhibitions, representing and selling her work from San Francisco to Paris.

Her clients include Fortune 500 executives and prestigious fashion collectors, as well as artistically minded and fashion-forward shoppers at design shows and art fairs. Her designs are known for their one-of-a-kind sophistication and high-fashion aesthetic.

About the Author: *I am an American Canadian citizen now living abroad in southwest Germany with my husband, twin daughters, and son. Living in Europe is a bucket list dream item that positively impacts my work, from the inspiration I see around me, to the new materials I have access to. Traveling and exposing myself to new environments and people has always been a big source of inspiration for my artworks, collections, and designs. I love felting with all my heart, and sharing my art with others is a source of great joy in my life.*

Acknowledgments

Editor: Cherie Zaslawsky
Main photographer: Michelle Bateman
Other photo credits:
Heidi Gress: Cover, pages 4, 7, 15, and 22
Florian Gurtner: *Weekend in Paris* photo shoot

Felting assistant: Hailey Frazier, thank you for assisting me in creating my *Weekend in Paris Collection* and for assisting with the photo shoot in Paris and for your contribution to this book.

A huge thank-you to my photographer Michelle Bateman, who accompanied me to the WollKnoll for every project photo shoot for this book. As a felt designer and professional photographer, she captured every detail of my work process for you to enjoy. She also gave me great insight into the content for this book.

Thank you to Andrea Graham, a felting friend, for giving me valuable input on various sections of my book.

Thank you to my global Felting Community, many of whom have become close friends over the years and have influenced my felting journey. Thank you to the countless felters in every corner of the world, who, by sharing their passion for felting online and in their felting circles, inspire other felt artists to create. It is amazing to be connected by such a transformative art and ancient tradition that has persisted and evolved over thousands of years.

WollKnoll, thank you for inviting me into your felting space and allowing me to photograph my projects in your studio! Thank you for your hospitality and contribution to my work.

Thank you to all of my clients and collectors and to those who follow and support my work.

Dedication

For my amazing husband, John, who encouraged me to write this book and has always supported my artistic dreams.
For my twin girls, Addie and Ellie, who inspire me daily to reach for more.
For Conrad, my son, whom I carried in pregnancy for the entire duration of writing this book. Your constant kicks were good reminders for me to stay focused.
For my mom, Renae Hill, and late grandpa, Stan Cramer, who gave me and my family the gift of creating art.
For my dad, Arden Hill, who taught me how to start and run my own business.
Last, but not least, for my siblings, who have always believed in my crazy dreams.